ORIGINAL SIN DEBUNKED

Solving the riddle of Romans 5:12

Gerald B. Shugart

Lulu Publishing | Morrisville, North Carolina

ORIGINAL SIN DEBUNKED

by

Gerald B. Shugart

Copyright, ©2020 by Gerald B. Shugart

FIRST EDITION

ISBN: 978-0-9856826-9-9

All rights reserved. No part of this book may be reproduced in any form without permission in writing, except in the case of brief quotations in specific Bible studies, critical articles or reviews.

All quoted sources and Bible translations are the property of their respective owners.

Formatting conducted by ShelfBloom ePress. Concerns about formatting, typographical errors, etc. should be sent to support@shelfbloom.com

DEDICATION

With gratitude I dedicate this book to my lovely wife Patti, who has been loving and supportive during our forty years of marriage.

Table of Contents

Chapter I | Original Sin Debunked	1
Chapter II | Solving the Riddle of Romans 5:12-21	19
Chapter III | Aurelius Augustine (354-430 A.D.)	38
Chapter IV | An Examination of the Natural Headship View of Original Sin	48
Chapter V | An Examination of the Federal Headship View of Original Sin	55
Chapter VI | Original Sin is an Offense to Human Reason	62
Chapter VII | Conclusion	68
Appendix #1 | "Born of Water and the Spirit"	75
Appendix #2 | "Law" or "the Law" at Romans 5:13?	83
Appendix #3 | Was Romans 5:12-14 a Riddle in the First Century?	87
Appendix #4 | There is None Righteous, No, Not One	90
Appendix #5 | The Flesh Lusteth Against the Spirit	93
Appendix #6 | By Nature the Children of Wrath	97
Appendix #7 | In Sin Did My Mother Conceive Me	99

Chapter I. Original Sin Debunked

Introduction

The theory of Original Sin according to the church at Rome can be summarized by the following statement:

"*Adam and Eve transmitted to their descendants human nature wounded by their own first sin and hence deprived of original holiness and justice; this deprivation is called 'original sin.'*" [1]

Calvinist R. C. Sproul writes that "*the condition of radical corruption, or total depravity, is the fallen state known as 'original sin'...The moral inability of fallen man is the core concept of the doctrine of total depravity or radical corruption.*" [2]

Calvinist Thomas R. Schreiner wrote that "*human beings enter into the world condemned and spiritually dead because of Adam's one sin.*" [3]

Chapter I. The Lord Jesus Was Made Like His Brethren in All Things

Now we will do a detailed study which will demonstrate that the proponents of the theory of Original Sin are in error. To start let us look at the following passage which speaks of the Lord Jesus Christ:

"*For verily he took not on him the nature of angels; but he took on him the seed of Abraham.* **Wherefore in all things it behoved him to be made like unto his brethren**, *that he might be a merciful and faithful high priest in things pertaining to God, to* *make reconciliation for the sins of the people*" (Heb.2:16-17).

In his commentary on this verse Matthew Poole wrote that "*To be made like unto his brethren;* **a man having a true body and soul like them in every thing**, *which was necessary to make him a complete Redeemer; agreeable to them in all things necessary to their nature, qualities, conditions, and affections; like them in sorrows, griefs, pains, death*" [*emphasis added*]. [4]

According to Poole the Lord Jesus' body and soul was just like the body and soul of every person.

Albert Barnes sees the same truth, writing that "*Wherefore in all things - In respect to his body; his soul; his rank and character. There was a propriety that he should be like them, and should partake of their nature.*" [5]

It defies reason to argue that all people emerge from the womb with a corrupted nature and spiritually dead despite the fact that the Scriptures reveal that the Lord Jesus was made like His brothers in "all things." However, that is exactly the argument that the advocates of the theory of Original Sin make.

1. God Created Mankind Upright

"*'Look,' says the Teacher, 'this is what I have discovered: Adding one thing to another to discover the scheme of things-- while I was still searching but not finding--I found one upright man among a thousand, but not one upright woman among them all. This only have I found:* **God created mankind upright, but they have gone in search of many schemes**'" (Eccl.7:25-29; NIV).

We can understand that here Solomon is speaking of the uprightness of "mankind" and not just the uprightness of only Adam and Eve. Mark Dunagan understands the same truth:

"*God made men upright*"-i.e. *morally good, God created men* *and women in His own image...God has given to every one the ability to recognize divine law as truth. This explains why Solomon found only one righteous man in a thousand. **The failure wasn't due to how God created people, rather, God created mankind upright**. Note the verse isn't saying that people are born inherently depraved, rather, after being born, after a period of childhood innocence, most people depart from God and search out excuses for not serving God*" [emphasis added]. [6]

Adam Clarke agrees with Dunagan, writing the following: "*Lo, this only have I found, that God hath made man upright - Whatever evil may be now found among men and women, it is not of God; **for God made them all upright**. This is a singular verse, and has been most variously translated:* **"Elohim has made mankind upright**, *and they have sought many computations*" [emphasis added]. [7]

Many of the early church leaders believed that all people have the power or ability to do good, as witnessed by the following words of Irenaeus:

"*Those who work it will receive glory and honor, **because they have done that which is good when they had it in their power not to do it**. But those who do not do it will receive the just judgment of God, **because they did not work good when they had it in their power to do so***" [emphasis added]. [8]

Clement of Alexander mirrors what Irenaeus said:

"***To obey or not is in our own power***, *provided we do not have the excuse of ignorance*" [emphasis added]. [9]

Tertullian speaks of a person's power to be obedient to the law:

"*I find, then, that man was constituted free by God. He was master of his own will and power...**For a law would not be imposed upon one who did not have in his power to render that obedience which is due to law***" [emphasis added]. [10]

We also read the following:

"*All the creatures that God made, he made very good...whoever wishes to may keep his commandments...everyone is given liberty of will*" [*emphasis added*]. [11]

2. Made in the Image of God

The following verse demonstrates that all people are made in the image of God:

"*For if the woman be not covered, let her also be shorn: but if it be a shame for a woman to be shorn or shaven, let her be covered. For a man indeed ought not to cover his head, forasmuch as **he is the image and glory of God**: but the woman is the glory of the man*" (1 Cor.11:7).

In this verse the Greek word translated "he is" the image and glory of God is in the "present tense" so the verse is not referring to just Adam being the image and glory of God. Adam Clarke wrote: "***He is the image and glory of God*** - *He is God's vicegerent in this lower world; and, by the authority which he has received from his Master, he is his representative among the creatures,* **and exhibits, more than any other part of the creation, the glory and perfections of the Creator**" [*emphasis added*]. [12]

We can see the same truth here:

"*Whoso sheddeth man's blood, by man shall his blood be shed: **for in the image of God made he man**"* (Gen.9:6).

The reason why all murderers are to be put to death is because those murdered are created in the image of God. What is said here would not make any sense if just Adam and Eve were created in the image of God. We also read the following which is in regard to the same truth:

"*Therewith bless we God, even the Father; and **therewith curse we men, which are made after the similitude of God**"*

(Jas.3:9).

The Greek word translated "curse we" is in the "present" tense so the words about being made after the similitude of God are describing all people and not just Adam and Eve.

Henry Morris wrote that "*This is a reference to Genesis 1:26-27. Even though scarred by thousands of years of sin and the curse, **man is still made in the image of God**, and should be respected as such*" [emphasis added]. [13]

Adam was created in the image of God and according to Him everything He made was "very good" (Gen.1:31). Since all people are created in the image or similitude of God all people emerge from the womb "very good."

That matches perfectly with the way that David said he was made:

"*For **you created my inmost being**; you knit me together in my mother's womb. **I praise you because I am fearfully and wonderfully made**; your works are wonderful, I know that full well*" (Ps.139:13-14; NIV).

No one in the history of Christendom has played a larger role in formulating the theory of Original Sin as Augustine of Hippo, and he wrote the following:

"*Our bodies would not have been born with defects, and there would have been no human monsters, if Adam had not corrupted our nature by his sin...The sickly and dying nature of the human body, proceeds from the lapse of the first man.*" [14]

What Augustine said here cannot possibly be correct because David said that he was "wonderfully made."

3. All People Are Born Spiritually Alive

In order to understand that all people are born spiritually alive let us look first at the following verse :

"*And you did he make alive, when **ye were dead through your trespasses and sins***" (Eph.2:1; ASV).

A note at Ephesians 2:5 in *The Scofield Study Bible* states that "***Spiritual death is the state of the natural or unregenerate person still in his sins (2:1)***, *alienated from the life of God (4:18-19), and destitute of the Spirit...*" [emphasis added]. [15]

In *The Pulpit Commentary* we read that "*the death ascribed to the Ephesians in their natural state is evidently **spiritual death**, and 'trespasses and sins,' **being in the dative seems to indicate the cause of death - 'dead through your trespasses and your sins' (R.V.)**"* [emphasis added]. [16]

From this we can understand that a person dies spiritually as a result or because of his own sin, and not as a result of Adam's sin.

In his commentary of the passage at Ephesians 2:1 R.C. Sproul writes that "*in this passage Paul speaks of the Spirit's work in 'quickening' us or regenerating us from our fallen condition. He uses the image of being 'made alive.' This is set in stark contrast to our former condition of being 'dead' in trespasses and sins. The sinner is not biologically dead. Indeed the natural man is very much alive. Corpses do not sin. **The death in view here is clearly spiritual death**"* [emphasis added] [17]

We also read the following commentary on Ephesians 2:1 in *The Expositor's Greek Testament*:

"*Here sin is that which makes dead--the cause of the death-state. In the kindred passage in Col. ii. 13 we have the same idea expressed*" [18]

With this in mind we will look at Colossians 2:13:

"*And you, **being dead through your trespasses and the uncircumcision of your flesh**, you, I say, did he make alive together with him, having forgiven us all our trespasses*" (Col.2:13; ASV).

In *Vincent's Word Studies* we read the following: "*In your sins...**the dative is instrumental, through or by***" [*emphasis added*]. [19]

At Colossians 2:13 Paul is telling these people that they are dead on account of or as a result of their own sins. And the "death" spoken of in the following passage must be in regard to a person's own sins resulting in spiritual death:

"*When tempted, no one should say, 'God is tempting me.' For God cannot be tempted by evil, nor does he tempt anyone; but each person is tempted when they are dragged away by their own evil desire and enticed. Then, after desire has conceived, it gives birth to sin; **and sin, when it is full-grown, gives birth to death***" (Jas.1:13-15).

It is a fact that in order for a person to die spiritually when he sins then that person must first be alive spiritually. And the following words of the Lord Jesus make it plain that once a person believes and is made alive spiritually he will never die spiritually:

"*I am the resurrection, and the life: he that believeth in me, though he were dead, yet shall he live: **And whosoever liveth and believeth in me shall never die***" (Jn.11:25-26).

Joseph Benson wrote the following commentary on John 11:26:

"*To the soul: he who, being united to Christ by faith, **lives a spiritual life by virtue of that union, shall never die; his spiritual life shall never be extinguished**, but perfected in eternal life*" [*emphasis added*]. [20]

The life which the Lord Jesus bestows on believers is spiritual life (Jn.3:6, Jn.6:63) and the believer will never die spiritually so the words of James at 1:13-15 cannot be in regard to believers dying spiritually. The only alternative is that all people die spiritually when they sin because all people emerge from the womb spiritually alive and not spiritually dead.

Despite the clear facts that a person dies spiritually as a result of his personal sins Thomas Schreiner writes that *"Our alienation and separation from God are due to Adam's sin, and thus we sin as a result of being born into the world separated from God's life. The notion that we are 'dead in trespasses and sins" (Eph.2:1; cf. Eph.2:5; Col. 2:13) should be interpreted similarly. The phrase does not mean that first we commit traspasses and sins and as a consequence die."* [21]

4. The Rebirth and Renewing of the Holy Spirit

In the following verse the Apostle Paul describes how he was saved by being made alive by the spirit:

"He saved us through the washing of rebirth and renewal by the Holy Spirit" (Titus 3:5; NIV).

Joseph Henry Thayer says that the Greek word translated 'rebirth' *"denotes **the restoration of a thing to its pristine state**, its renovation"* [emphasis added]. [22]

The word "rebirth" is translated from the Greek word *paliggenesia*, which is the combination of *palin* and *genesis*.

Palin means *"joined to verbs of all sorts, it denotes renewal or **repetition of the action**"* [emphasis added]. [23]

According to BDAG, *palin* refers *"**to repetition in the same (or similar) manner**, again, once more, anew of something a pers. has already done"* [emphasis added]. [24]

Genesis means *"used of **birth**, nativity."* [emphasis added]. [25]

So when we combine the two words the meaning is a repetition of a birth. Therefore, when Paul used the Greek word translated "rebirth" to describe his salvation experience he was speaking of a repetition of a birth.

It is obvious that the reference is not to a "physical" rebirth, or the repetition of one's physical birth. Paul could only be speaking of a repetition of a spiritual birth. And the words that follow make it certain that the "birth" of which Paul is referring to is a "spiritual" birth--"*renewal of the Holy Spirit.*"

Since the renewal of the Holy Spirit is in regard to being made alive spiritually then the previous birth of the Spirit must also be in regard to being made alive spiritually by the Holy Spirit. In other words, since a person is "rebirthed" by the Holy Spirit then that means that one must have previously been born of the Holy Spirit. That happens at conception.

In the following passage Paul speaks of being "alive" before he sinned:

"*For **I was alive** without the law once: but when the commandment came, sin revived, and **I died**. And the commandment, which was ordained to life, **I found to be unto death**. For sin, taking occasion by the commandment, deceived me, and by **it slew me***" (Ro.7:9-11).

Paul is not speaking of "physical" death because he was alive physically when he wrote those words. He is speaking about breaking one of the Ten Commandments (v.7) and it was that which resulted in his "spiritual death."

In his commentary on this passage John A. Witmer writes, "***As a result Paul 'died' spiritually** (cf. 6:23a) under the sentence of judgment by the Law he had broken...so this sin deceived him...and 'put' him 'to death' (lit., 'killed' him), **not physically but spiritually**" [emphasis added].* [26]

Since Paul died spiritually when he sinned then he was alive spiritually prior to his sin and therefore he was born of the Spirit when he was conceived in the womb. The Lord Jesus said:

"*That which is born of the flesh is flesh; **and that which is born of the Spirit is spirit**" (Jn.3:6).

Besides that, the Scriptures declare that people are created by the LORD when He sends forth His spirit:

"***Thou sendest forth thy spirit, they are created****: and thou renewest the face of the earth*" (Ps.104.30).

Elihu told Job the following:

"***The Spirit of God hath made me****, and the breath of the Almighty hath given me life*" (Job.33:4).

The fact that all people emerge from the womb spiritually alive completely destroys the theory of Original Sin because according to that theory all people are dead spiritually when they come into the world at birth. Thomas R. Schreiner writes that "*human beings enter the world spiritually dead (and physical death will follow in due course) because of Adam's sin. Human beings do not enter into the world in a neutral state. They are 'dead upon arrival' because of Adam's sin!*" [27]

For more information concerning the birth of water and the spirit please go to Appendix #1.

5. The Kingdom Belongs to Little Children

The following words of the Lord Jesus about "little children" prove that He did not believe that little children enter the world with a fallen nature:

"*Then people brought little children to Jesus for him to place his hands on them and pray for them. But the disciples rebuked them. Jesus said, 'Let the little children come to me, and do not hinder them,* **for the kingdom of heaven belongs to such as these**'" (Mt.19:13-14; NIV).

According to the theory of Original Sin infants and little children emerged from the womb totally depraved and therefore cannot enter the kingdom of God in their fallen state but the Lord says that the kingdom belongs to them. At another place we see the Lord Jesus speaking about children and here the same truth can be seen:

"*At the same time came the disciples unto Jesus, saying, Who is the greatest in the kingdom of heaven? And Jesus called a little child unto him, and set him in the midst of them, And said, Verily I say unto you,* **Except ye be converted, and become as little children, ye shall not enter into the kingdom of heaven**. *Whosoever therefore shall humble himself as this little child, the same is greatest in the kingdom of heaven*" (Mt.18:1-4).

If the idea of Original Sin is correct then we must stand reason on its head and imagine that the Lord Jesus was teaching that unless we become deprived of holiness we cannot enter into the kingdom of heaven! That is patently ridiculous and common sense dictates that the Lord Jesus did not believe that infants come into the world tainted with Original Sin .

We can also see that children are also described as being "an heritage of the Lord":

"*Lo, children are an heritage of the LORD: and the fruit of the womb is his reward*" (Ps.127:3).

Despite these facts Rome teaches that an infant must be baptized with water to be freed from the power of darkness:

"*Born with a fallen human nature and tainted by original sin, children also have need of the new birth in Baptism to be freed from the power of darkness and brought into the realm of the freedom of the children of God, to which all men are called*" [28]

6. Moral Inability?

R. C. Sproul writes that "*The moral inability of fallen man is the core concept of the doctrine of total depravity or radical corruption.*" [29]

Of course the Scriptures declare in no uncertain terms that no one has ever obtained eternal life as a result of his own works but the question which concerns us is whether or not it is theoretically possible.

If the Scriptures teach that a person can, at least in theory, obtain eternal life by his own works then it cannot be denied that every person does in fact have the moral ability to keep God's law. After all, if people do not have the ability to obtain eternal life by their own works then it is impossible, even in theory, that they can. In the second chapter of the book of *Romans* Paul reveals that a man can theoretically obtain eternal life by his "deeds" or by his "works":

"*But after thy hardness and impenitent heart treasurest up unto thyself wrath against the day of wrath and revelation of the righteous judgment of God;* **Who will render to every man according to his deeds***: To them who* **by patient continuance in well doing seek for glory and honour and immortality, eternal life***: But unto them that are contentious, and do not obey the truth, but obey unrighteousness, indignation and wrath, Tribulation and anguish, upon every soul of man that doeth evil, of the Jew first, and also of the Gentile*" (Ro.2:5-9).

In his remarks on this passage Thomas R. Schreiner writes that "*The main purpose of this section is to demonstrate that the Jews fall short of God's righteousness. Nonetheless, one must still account for the assertion that those who do good works will be granted eternal life.* **Probably the dominant interpretation is that these verses are hypothetical.** *Eternal life would be given if one did good works and kept the law perfectly, but no one does the requisite good works, and thus all deserve punishment...At this stage in the argument of Romans, however,* **it is impossible to argue conclusively against the hypothetical interpretation.**" [emphasis added]. [30]

In his commentary on this passage Douglas J. Moo writes that "*Verses 7 and 8 outline the two possible outcomes of God rendering to 'each' according to works. On the one hand, to 'those who by their persistence in good works and seeking glory and honor and immorality' he will 'render' eternal life.* **Paul's suggestion that a person's 'good work' might lead to eternal life** *seems strange in the light of his teaching elsewhere*" [*emphasis added*]. *31*

Both Schreiner and Moo understand that Paul is saying that it is at least theoretically possible for a person to obtain eternal life by law-keeping. And of course that teaching of Paul sounds strange to those who believe that a person emerges from the womb spiritually dead and unable to do the necessary good works which could lead to eternal life. However, those who do not believe in the dogma of Original Sin, men like Sir Robert Anderson, teach that man has the ability to continue in well doing:

"*Therefore also is it that **while 'patient continuance in well doing' is within the human capacity**, Rom. 2:6-11 applies to all whether with or without a divine revelation...**The dogma of the moral depravity of man, and irremediable, cannot be reconciled with divine justice in punishing sin.** If by the law of his fallen nature man were incapable of doing right, it would be clearly inequitable to punish him for doing wrong. **If the Fall had made him crooked-backed, to punish him for not standing upright, would be worthy of an unscrupulous and cruel tyrant. But we must distinguish between theological dogma and divine truth.** That man is without excuse is the clear testimony of Holy Writ*" [*emphasis added*]. *32*

The Apostle Paul says that it is the doers of the law who shall be justified:

"*For not the hearers of the law are just before God, but **the doers of the law shall be justified***" (Ro.2:13).

Moo understand that it is at least theoretically possible for the doers of the law to be justified, writing that "*he (Paul) upholds faithful obedience to God, or to the law as a **'theoretical'** means of obtaining justification (cf. 2:13; 7:10)*" [*emphasis added*]. *33*

Schreiner admits that if anyone did keep the law then that person would be justified in the eyes of the LORD:

> "*What I have been arguing is that the reason works of law do not justify is that no one can observe what the law says. **If anyone could obey the law, then he or she would be justified***" [*emphasis added*]. [34]

If a person is born spiritually dead, as Schreiner asserts, then no amount of law-keeping could possibly bring eternal life or justification because once a person is spiritually dead due to his own sin then he must be born again of the Spirit in order to enter into the Kingdom of God (John 3:5). Therefore, we can understand that people do not enter the world spiritually dead because the Scriptures reveal that in theory a person can obtain eternal life by his own deeds or works.

End Notes

1. *The Catechism of the Catholic Church,* #417; Accesssed October 12, 2018, http://www.vatican.va/archive/ccc_css/archive/catechism/p1s2c1p7.htm

2. R.C.Sproul, *What is Reformed Theology?* (Grand Rapids: Baker Books, 1997), 121, 128.

3. Thomas R. Schreiner, "Original Sin and Original Death," in *Adam, The Fall, and Original sin* ed. Hans Madueme and Michael Reeves (Grand Rapids: Baker Academic, 2014), 276.

4. Matthew Poole, *Matthew Poole's Commentary*; Accessed August 15, 2018, http://biblehub.com/commentaries/poole/hebrews/2.htm.

5. Albert Barnes, *Notes on the Bible by Albert Barnes*; Accessed August 15, 2018, http://biblehub.com/commentaries/barnes/hebrews/2.htm.

6. Mark Dunagan, *Commentaries on the Bible*, "Commentary on Ecclesiastes 7:29; Accessed August 18, 2018, https://www.studylight.org/commentaries/dun/ecclesiastes-7.html.

7. Adam Clarke, *The Adam Clarke Commentary,*; Accessed August 18,2018, https://www.studylight.org/commentaries/acc/ecclesiastes-7.html.

8. *The Ante-Nicene Fathers*, ed. Alexander Roberts and James Donaldson,1885-1887; repr. 10 vols. (Peabody,

MA: Hendrickson, 1994), Volume 1, 519.

9. *Ibid.*, Volume 2, 353.

10. *Ibid.*, Volume 3, 300-301.

11. *Ibid.*, "Disputation of Archelaus and Manes," Volume 6, 204-205.

12. Adam Clarke, *Commentary on the Bible*, Accessed September 8, 2018, https://biblehub.com/commentaries/clarke/1_corinthians/11.htm

13. Henry Morris, *Defender's Study Bible*; Accessed September 8,2018, http://www.icr.org/books/defenders/8530/

14. G.F. Wiggers, An Historical Presentation of Augustinism and Pelagianism From the Original Sources (Andover, MA: Gould, Newman & Saxton, 1840), 97.

15. *The Scofield Study Bible; King James Version* (New York: Oxford University Press, 2003), 1557.

16. *The Pulpit Commentary*, Accessed September 2, 2018, http://biblehub.com/commentaries/pulpit/ephesians/2.htm

17. R.C. Sproul, *What is Reformed Theology?* (Grand Rapids: Baker Books, 1997), 129.

18. *The Expositor's Greek Testament*, ed. W. Robertson Nicoll, volume III, (New York and London: Hodder and Stoughton), 283.

19. Marvin R. Vincent, *Vincent's Word Studies*; Accessed August 28, 2018, http://biblehub.com/commentaries/vws/colossians/2.htm

20. Joseph Benson, *Benson Commentary on the Old and*

New Testaments; Accessed September 8, 2018, https://biblehub.com/commentaries/benson/john/11.htm

21. Thomas R. Schreiner, *Romans* (Grand Rapids: Baker Academic, 1998), 276.

22. Joseph Henry Thayer, *A Greek - English Lexicon of the New Testament* (Grand Rapids: Baker Book House, 1977), 474.

23. *Ibid.,* 475.

24. Walter Bauer, *A Greek-English Lexicon of the New Testament and Other Early Christian Literature*, 3rd ed., ed. Frederick William Danker (Chicago: University of Chicago Press, 2000), 752.

25. Joseph Henry Thayer, *A Greek - English Lexicon of the New Testament*, 112.

26. John A. Witmer, "Romans," in *The Bible Knowledge Commentary; New Testament,* ed. John F. Walvoord and Roy B. Zuck (Colorado Springs: Chariot Victor Publishing, 1983), 467.

27. Thomas R. Schreiner, *Adam, the Fall, and Original Sin*, 282-83.

28. *The Catechism of the Catholic Church,* #1250; Accesssed October 24, 2018, http://www.vatican.va/archive/ccc_css/archive/catechism/p1s2c1p7.htm

29. R.C.Sproul, *What is Reformed Theology?*, 128.

30. Thomas R. Schreiner, *Romans*, (Grand Rapids: Baker Academic, 1998), 114-15.

31. Douglas J. Moo, *The Epistle to the Romans* (Grand Rapids: Wm. B. Eedermans Publishing Co., 1996), 136-7.

32. Sir Robert Anderson, "Sin and Judgment to Come," *The Fundamentals: A Testimony to the Truth*; Volume VI (Chicago: Testimony Publishing Co., 1910), 42-3, 38-9.

33. Douglas J. Moo, *The Epistle to the Romans*, 141.

34. Thomas R. Schreiner, *Romans*, 173.

Chapter II. Solving the Riddle of Romans 5:12-21

Thomas Schreiner says Romans 5:12-19 serves as the basis for denying or affirming original sin:

"***Whether Scripture teaches what is traditionally called 'original sin' depends significantly on the exegesis of Romans 5:12-19.*** *Since the days of Augustine, the interpretation of this text functions as the basis for denying or affirming original sin.* ***I will argue in this chapter that the most plausible reading of Romans 5:12-19, both exegetically and theologically, supports the doctrine of original sin and original death***" [emphasis added]. [1]

Let us look at the following verse, paying particular attention to that which is in "bold":

"*For this cause, even as by one man sin entered into the world, and by sin death;* ***and thus death passed upon all men, for that all have sinned.***"(Ro.5:12; DBY).

Schreiner says that the "death" under discussion is caused by a person's own individual sinning, writing that "*5:12cd teaches that death spread to all because all sinned...Paul regularly argues in Romans 5 and 6 that sin begets death, context supports the interpretation, 'and so death spread to all men because all sinned'...to paraphrase:* ***'death spread to all people because all sinned individually'*** " [emphasis added]. [2]

Douglas J. Moo, another defender of the theory of Original Sin, writes that "*Paul certainly uses the verb 'sin' regularly to denote voluntary sinful acts committed by individuals; and this is what most commentators think that this same word, in the same tense as is used here (aorist), designates in 3:23: that all people, 'in their own persons,' commit sins.* ***Probably a majority of*** *contemporary scholars interpret 5:12d, then, to assert that the death of each person (v.12c) is directly caused by that person's own individual sinning*" [*emphasis added*]. ³

A majority of contemporary scholars agree that the "death" spoken of by Paul at Romans 5:12c is directly caused by the sins which individuals commit. And when we compare the following two verses it becomes clear that Romans 5:12 is indeed speaking about individual sins:

"*For this cause, even as by one man sin entered into the world, and by sin death; and thus death passed upon all men, for that **all have sinned (pas hamartano)***"(Ro.5:12; DBY).

"*For **all have sinned (pas hamartano)**, and come short of the glory of God*" (Ro.3:23).

1. Personal Sins Result in Spiritual Death

The following passage speaks of individual sins and the results which follow:

"*Behold, the LORD's hand is not shortened, that it cannot save; neither his ear heavy, that it cannot hear. **But your iniquities have separated between you and your God**, and your sins have hid his face from you, that he will not hear. For your hands are defiled with blood, and your fingers with iniquity; your lips have spoken lies, your tongue hath muttered perverseness*" (Isa.59:1-3).

From this we know that when a person sins that sin separates him from God.

Schreiner understands that this separation is referring to spiritual death:

"*Both Adam and Eve when they sinned **died spiritually in that they were separated from God**"* [*emphasis added*]. ⁴

In his comments on the "death" mentioned at Romans 5:12, Moo wrote the following:

"But what does Paul mean by death here? He may refer to physical death only, since 'death' in verse 14 seems to have this meaning. But the passsage goes on to contrast death with eternal life (v. 21). Moreover, in verses 16 and 18 Paul uses 'condemnation' in the same way that he uses 'death' here. **These points suggest that Paul is referring to 'spiritual' death: the estrangement from God that is a result of sin***, and that, if not healed through Christ, will lead to 'eternal' death"* [*emphasis added*]. [5]

In the first chapter evidence from the Scriptures was given which demonstrates that it is personal sins which result in spiritual death and not the one sin of Adam..

2. All Died Spiritually So All Were Previously Alive Spiritually

Now let us look at the following verse again:

"For this cause, even as by one man sin entered into the world, and by sin death; **and thus death passed upon all men, for that all have sinned**" (Ro.5:12; DBY).

Paul is saying that spiritual death passed upon "all" people because "all" have sinned. That can only mean that at some point in time "all" people are spiritually alive. The word "death" means "end of life" so we can understand that before "all" people die spiritually they were "all" alive spiritually before they sinned. And the only way that "all" people can be spiritually alive is because they all emerge from the womb spiritually alive.

This fact alone proves that the theory of Original Sin is false.

Schreiner's teaching contradicts the simple fact that all people are born in a state which can only be described as being spiritually alive when he writes that *"human beings enter into the world condemned and spiritually dead because of Adam's one sin...human beings do not enter into the world in a neutral state. They are 'dead upon arrival' because of Adam's sin."* [6]

3. The Riddle

In his book *Original Sin: Illuminating the Riddle* Henri Blocher writes the following:

"Romans 5:12ff. fully deserves the appellation 'sedes doctrinae,' the 'seat' or 'fundament' of the doctrine of original sin. Whenever this doctrine is discussed, Romans 5 is in the eye of the storm." [7]

Although Blocher characterizes Original Sin as a "riddle" it is actually the following passage which the proponents of the theory of Original Sin fail to understand and so to them it is a riddle:

"For this cause, even as by one man sin entered into the world, and by sin death; and thus death passed upon all men, for that all have sinned: for until law sin was in the world; but sin is not put to account when there is no law; but death reigned from Adam until Moses, even upon those who had not sinned in the likeness of Adam's transgression, who is the figure of him to come" (Ro.5:12-14; DBY).

Blocher says that Paul's explanation about how Adam communicated a sinful bent to his posterity should be expected in this passage but it is not found there:

"**It is rather strange that the core idea**, *or the hinge of the apostle's purpoted logic - that Adam communicated the sinful bent to his posterity -* **should not be expressed at all in the passage**. *It 'might' be explicit; undoubtedly, Paul did share the opinion;* **yet how surprising that he should not include something here, of all places, to make it clear!**" [*emphasis added*]. [8]

Moo writes that Paul said nothing about how the sin of Adam resulted in the death of everyone:

"*Paul says nothing explicitly about 'how' the sin of one man, Adam, has resulted in death for everyone;* **nor has he made clear the connection between Adam's sin (v. 12a) and the sin of all people (v. 12d).**" [*emphasis added*]. [9]

Besides that Moo says that "*Paul in v.12 asserts that all people sin on their own account; and in vv.18-19 he claims that they all die because of Adam's sin.* **Paul does not resolve these two perspectives; and we do wrong to try to force a resolution that Paul himseslf never made**" [*emphasis added*]. [10]

The advocates of the theory of Original Sin did in fact force a resolution and according to that resolution all people emerge from the womb with a corrupted nature. That idea is contradicted by the fact that all people emerge from the womb spiritually alive. When the riddle is solved we will see that the solution remains consistent with the fact that people are born into this world spiritually alive.

4. The Clue that Solves the Riddle

When we examine what is in "bold" in the following passage we will see that Paul does tell us exactly how spiritual death came upon all people when they sin and that evidence will be the clue to understanding in what way Adam's sin resulted in the death of all people when they sin:

"*For this cause, even as by one man sin entered into the world, and by sin death; and thus death passed upon all men, for that all have sinned:* **for until law sin was in the world; but sin is not put to account when there is no law; but death reigned from Adam until Moses**, *even upon those who had not sinned in the likeness of Adam's transgression, who is the figure of him to come*" (Ro.5:12-14; DBY).

Verse 13 begins with the Greek word *gar* (which is translated 'for') and one of the meanings of that word is "*it adduces the Cause or gives the Reason of a preceding statement or opinion.*" [11]

From this we can understand that verses 13-14 will give the clue as to why Paul said that Adam's sin was responsible for bringing death unto all who sin. The "law" referred to at verse 13 can only be the "law" which Paul mentioned earlier in the same epistle and was the only law in effect between Adam and Moses, the law which is written in the heart of which the conscience bears witness:

"*For when the Gentiles, which have not the law, do by nature the things contained in the law, these, having not the law, are a law unto themselves:* **Which shew the work of the law written in their hearts, their conscience also bearing witness**" (Ro.2:14-15).

For more information concerning this subject please go to Appendix #2.

Thomas Schreiner understands that those who lived between Adam and Moses were judged for violating the law inscribed in their hearts:

"*Those who lived in the era between Adam and Moses,*" he says, "*were accountable for their sins, so that they were condemned because they violated God's moral norms. Their sin was counted against them and thus they were judged. Paul himself teaches the same truth in 2:12, when he claims that 'all those who sinned without the law will also perish without the law.'...***Gentiles who did not know or possess the Mosaic law were judged for violating the law inscribed on their hearts (2:14-15)***...Romans 2:12 is of paramount importance, for it prevents us from adopting a mistaken view of 5:12-14*" [emphasis added]. [12]

In his commentary on Romans 5:13 we can see that Albert Barnes came to the same conclusion:

"But sin is not imputed - Is not charged against people, or they are not held guilty of it where there is no law. This is a self-evident proposition, for sin is a violation of law; and if there is no law, there can be no wrong. Assuming this as a self-evident proposition, **the connection is, that there must have been a law of some kind; a 'law written on their hearts,'** *since sin was in the world, and people could not be charged with sin, or treated as sinners, unless there was some law"* [emphasis added]. [13]

From this we can understand that all people who lived between Adam and Eve died spiritually when they sinned against their conscience. And in some way Adam's sin was responsible for all people having a conscience. With this evidence to guide us it is not difficult to solve the riddle.

5. The Riddle Solved

The solution as to how Adam's sin was responsible for all people dying spiritually when they sinned is found here in "bold":

"And the LORD God said, Behold, the man is become as one of us, **to know good and evil***: and now, lest he put forth his hand, and take also of the tree of life, and eat, and live for ever"* (Gen.3:22).

When Adam sinned by eating of the tree of the knowledge of good and evil he received a conscience. And then all of his posterity were made in his image, also having a conscience:

"And Adam lived an hundred and thirty years, **and begat a son in his own likeness, and after his image***; and called his name Seth"* (Gen.5:3).

If Adam would have remained in a state of innocence and had not sinned then he would not have received this consciousness of the law written in his heart and therefore his descendants would not have received this consciousness so any sin they committed would not have been counted against them because "sin is not imputed when there is no law." Therefore, none of them would have died spiritually when they sinned since they would not have had a conscience.

In his comments on these verses John Wesley wrote that after eating of the forbidden tree Adam and Eve received a conscience:

"***The Eyes of them both were opened - The eyes of their consciences****; their hearts smote them for what they had done. Now, when it was too late, they saw the happiness they were fallen from, and the misery they were fallen into. They saw God provoked, his favour forfeited, his image lost*" [emphasis added]. [14]

Clarence Larkin wrote: "*Adam and Eve had no conscience before the 'Fall.'* **Conscience is a knowledge of 'Good' and 'Evil,' and this Adam and Eve did not have until they had their eyes opened by eating of the 'Fruit' of the 'Tree of the Knowledge of Good and Evil'**" [emphasis added]. [15]

Renald E. Showers writes that "**Genesis 3:5 and 22 indicate that mankind obtained its awareness of good and evil as a result of eating the forbidden fruit. In other words, the human conscience began when man rebelled against God**...*Paul indicated that the conscience is the awareness of good and evil which exists inside human beings. It condemns people internally when they do something in the category of evil, and it commends them internally when they do something in the category of good*" [emphasis added]. [16]

We also read the following in *The Popular Encyclopedia of Bible Prophecy*:

"*The Edenic covenant is tied to the dispensation of innocence, whereby God tested man to see if he would live by God's conditions. God told man not to eat of the fruit of the tree of the knowledge of good and evil (Genesis 2:17). The dispensation ended in man's failure--Eve was deceived (1 Timothy 2:14) and Adam deliberately disobeyed. As a result, the first man had personal and experiental knowledge of good and evil. **What*** *seemed like a simple, limited act of eating fruit ended in a broad, conscious knowledge of right and wrong. In the next dispensation, the descendants of Adam were responsible for this new awareness of sin*" [*emphasis added*]. [17]

Again, if Adam would have obeyed the LORD then he would have remained in a state of "innocence" so therefore "law" would not have come upon his descendants: "*when there is no law, sin is not imputed.*" This principle is explained in the following verse:

"*Therefore to him that knoweth to do good, and doeth it not, to him it is sin*" (Jas.4:17).

God will not impute sin into a person's account unless that person first knows the difference between what is good and what is not.

Therefore we can understand that if the people who lived between the time of Adam until Moses had no inborn knowledge of what is good and what is evil then sin would not have been imputed into their accounts because "*when there is no law sin is not imputed.*" And since Adam was responsible for all people having a conscience then in an indirect way Adam's sin lead to the spiritual death of all men because all men die spiritually as a result of their own sin against their conscience.

6. Romans 5:15

Next, we will see that the verses which follow give even more evidence that the theory of Original Sin is contradicted by the Scriptures.

"*But not as the offence, so also is the free gift. For if through the offence of one **many** be dead, much more the grace of God, and the gift by grace, which is by one man, Jesus Christ, hath abounded unto many*" (Ro.5:15).

Here we read that because of the offence of Adam "many"

died but not "all." This verse alone refutes the teaching of Original Sin because according to those who promote the idea of Original Sin "all" people emerge from the womb spiritually dead. In this verse the Greek word translated "many" is used twice and the second time it is used it is impossible that the reference is to "all":

*"But not as the offence, so also is the free gift. For if through the offence of one **many** be dead, much more the grace of God, and the gift by grace, which is by one man, Jesus Christ, hath abounded unto **many**"* (Ro.5:15).

It is a fact that the second time the word "many" is used it cannot possibly be referring to "all" because the gift by grace has not abounded unto "all." Only those with faith receive the gift and not all people have faith. In the passage starting at verse 15 until verse 19 we see Paul employ a figure of speech called Parallelism:

*"**Parallelism ; or, Parallel Lines.** The repetition of similiar, synonymous, or opposite thoughts or words in parallel or successive lines."* [18]

John Murray recognized this same literary device, writing that *"Adam is the type of the one to come (v. 14). Adam as the one is parallel to Jesus Christ as the one (v. 17). The one trespass unto condemnation is parallel to the one righteousness unto justification (v. 18). The disobedience of the one is parallel to the obedience of one (v.18)."* [19]

In order to be logically consistent in regard to this parallelism the Greek word translated "many" cannot have one meaning the first time it is used and then have an entirely different meaning the second time it is used. Therefore, it is impossible that Paul is saying that as a result of Adam's sin "all" have died spiritually.

The reason why Paul says that "many" die and not "all" is because it is only those who sin who experience spiritual death-- *"and thus death passed upon all men, **for that all have sinned**"* (Ro.5:12; DBY).

Since children have not sinned they have not died spiritually so that is why Paul says that this death passed unto "many" and not "all." The following verse gives more evidence to support this truth:

"*Moreover your little ones, which ye said should be a prey, and your children, **which in that day had no knowledge between good and evil, they shall go in thither, and unto them will I give it, and they shall possess it***" (Deut.1:39).

Jack S.Deere writes that "*God seems to acknowledge a so-called 'age of accountability' for **children**. Apparently children are not held accountable by God until they are aware of the difference between **good** and **bad**.*" [20]

Children are not held responsible for any sin until they can tell the difference between good and evil:

"*Therefore to him that knoweth to do good, and doeth it not, to him it is sin*" (Jas.4:17).

Therefore, we can understand that since little children do not sin and do not experience spiritual death then that explains why Paul said that "many" but not "all" experience spiritual death.

According to the theory of Original Sin "all" people emerge from the womb spiritually dead so Schreiner says that in this verse "many" means "all":

"*The word 'many' here certainly means 'all,' as subsequent verses attest. No room is allowed for exceptions. All of humanity, apart from Christ, died because Adam sinned.*" [21]

Now we will address the verses which Schreiner asserts teach that all people die spiritually as a result of Adam's sin.

7. Romans 5:18

*"Therefore as by the offence of one judgment came upon all men to condemnation; even so **by the righteousness of one the free gift came upon all men unto justification of life**"* (Ro.5:18; KJV).

A better translation is found here:

*"so then as it was by one offence **towards** all men to condemnation, so by one righteousness **towards** all men for justification of life"* (Romans 5:18; DBY).

John Witmer wrote that *"The provision in the one righteous act, therefore, **is potential** and it comes to the entire human race **as the offer and opportunity which are applied only to 'those who receive' (v. 17)**"* [*emphasis added*]. [22]

Here is the offer and opportunity which appeared to all people: *"For the grace of God that bringeth salvation hath appeared to all men"* (Titus 2:11). The grace of God that brings salvation is the gospel of grace and the LORD's intent is that all people should believe that gospel which results in the free gift unto justification of life but not all believe the gospel.

In his comments on Romans 5:18 Sir Robert Anderson wrote,

*"As by one act of sin judgment came unto all men to condemnation, even so through one act of righteousness the free gift came unto men to justification of life.' **Not that all men are in fact made righteous--that is for the many, not for all--but that such was the direction and tendency of the grace**"* [*emphasis added*].[23]

In his comments on verse 18 John Nelson Darby differentiates between the intention (scope) of the action from its actual application: *"In Verse 18 the general argument is resumed in a very abstract way. 'By one offence,' he says, 'towards all for condemnation, even so by one accomplished righteousness (or act of righteousness) towards all men, for justification of life.* **One offence bore in its bearing, so to speak, referred to all, and so it was with the one act of righteousness. This is the scope of the action in itself. Now for the application: for as by the disobedience of one man (only) many are constituted sinners, so by the obedience of one (only) many are constituted righteous"** [*emphasis added*]. [24]

The "scope" of the one offense towards all people to condemnation is that all people will be condemned and die spiritually when they sin against their consciences. But since infants and young children do not yet have a fully developed conscience they are not held accountable until they are aware of the difference between good and bad. So Darby was correct when he wrote, *"or as by the disobedience of one man (only) many are constituted sinners."*

This demonstrates that Schreiner was in error when he asserted that Romans 5:18 teaches that "all" people are condemned as a result of the sin of Adam.

8. Romans 5:19

*"For as by one man's disobedience **many** were made sinners, so by the obedience of one shall **many** be made righteous"* (Ro.5:19).

Here we read that "many" will be made righteous. And since not "all" people will be made righteous then it is impossible that the word "many" refers to all people. Five times Paul contrasts Adam with the Lord Jesus at Romans 5:15-19 and the sustained parallelism in these verses forbids the idea that when the word "many" is used in the first instance it means "all" and the second time it is used it doesn't mean "all" but instead only "many."

9. Romans 5:20-21

"Moreover the law entered, that the offence might abound. But where sin abounded, grace did much more abound: That as sin hath reigned unto death, even so might grace reign through righteousness unto eternal life by Jesus Christ our Lord" (Ro.5:20-21).

Previously Paul had been speaking of the law written in the heart of all men of which the conscience bears witness. But now he speaks of the Law given by Moses and he says that law "entered that the offense might abound" or increase. How did the giving of the law result in the offense increasing?

The law written in the heart of every person is limited in some respects because it does not reveal all of the LORD's demands for personal righteousness. In the following verse Paul says that he wouldn't have known that coveting is a sin unless he had been given the following commandment found in the Law of Moses:

"What shall we say then? Is the law sin? God forbid. Nay, I had not known sin, but by the law: for I had not known lust, except the law had said, **Thou shalt not covet***"* (Ro.7:7).

Physical Death and Spiritual Death?

Schreiner says that the words "eternal life" found in verse 21 indicate that the death cannot be restricted to physical death because it must also be in regard to "spiritual death: *"The death introduced by Adam is conjoined with 'condemnation' (vv.16, 18), and it is also contrasted with 'eternal life' (v.21). Thus it can hardly be restricted to physical death...I am not suggesting that physical death and spiritual death can ultimately be separated, for the former is the culmination and outworking of the latter."* [25]

Even though Schreiner asserts that physical death and spiritual death cannot be separated the facts say otherwise. People die spiritually when they sin but people die physically because they have been denied the very thing which would allow them to live forever in their physical bodies--the Tree of Life:

*"And the LORD God said, Behold, the man is become as one of us, to know good and evil: and now, **lest he put forth his hand, and take also of the tree of life, and eat, and live for ever: Therefore the LORD God sent him forth from the garden of Eden**, to till the ground from whence he was taken. So he drove out the man; and **he placed at the east of the garden of Eden Cherubims, and a flaming sword which turned every way, to keep the way of the tree of life**"* (Gen.3:22-25).

From this we can see that in order for Adam to live forever it was necessary for him to eat of the Tree of Life. And the same can be said of all of his posterity. Since the way to the Tree of Life has been denied to all of Adam's descendants then people die physically because they cannot eat of that tree. As a result of that people die physically:

"And as it is appointed unto men once to die, but after this the judgment" (Heb.9:27).

Therefore, the "death" spoken of in the following verse in "bold" can only be referring to spiritual death:

*"Wherefore, as by one man sin entered into the world, and death by sin; **and so death passed upon all men, for that all have sinned**"* (Ro.5:12).

Since all people die spiritually when they sin then all people must have first been alive spiritually before they sinned. And the only way that could possibly happen is because all people emerge from the womb spiritually alive.

That fact alone proves that the theory of Original Sin cannot possibly be correct.

End Notes

1. Thomas R. Schreiner, *Adam, the Fall, and Original Sin*, 271.
2. *Ibid.*, 274, 280.
3. Douglas J. Moo, "Sin in Paul," in *Fallen: A Theology of Sin*, ed. Christoper W. Morgan and Robert A. Peterson (Wheaton IL: Crossway, 2013), 122-3.
4. Thomas R. Schreiner, *Adam, the Fall, and Original Sin*, 272.
5. Douglas Moo, *Fallen: A Theology of Sin*, 121.
6. Thomas R. Schreiner, *Adam, the Fall, and Original Sin*, 283.
7. Henri Blocher, *Original Sin: Illuminating the Riddle* (Downers Grove, IL: InterVarsity Press, 1997), 63.
8. *Ibid.*, 66.
9. Douglas J. Moo, *Fallen: A Theology of Sin*, 122.
10. Douglas J. Moo, *The Epistle to the Romans* (Grand Rapids: William B. Eerdmans Publishing Co., 1996), 324.
11. John Henry Thayer, *A Greek-English Lexicon of the New Testament* (Grand Rapids: Baker Book House, 1977), 109.
12. Thomas R. Schreiner, *Adam, the Fall and Original Sin*, 279-280.
13. Albert Barnes, *Notes on the Bible*, Commentary on Romans 5; Accessed August 14, 2008, http://www.sacred-texts.com/bib/cmt/barnes/rom005.htm

14. John Wesley, *John Wesley's notes on the Bible*; Accessed August 14, 2018, https://www.biblestudytools.com/commentaries/wesleys-explanatory-notes/genesis/genesis-3.html

15. Clarence Larkin, *Rightly Dividing The Word* [Rev. Clarence Larkin Est.], 19.

16. Renald E. Showers, *The Second Dispensation*, Ankerberg Theological Research Institute; Accessed August 11, 2008, https://www.jashow.org/articles/general/dispensational-theology-part-3/

17. *The Popular Encyclopedia of Bible Prophecy*, ed.Tim LaHaye & Ed Hindson, (Eugene: Harvest House, 2004), 86.

18. *The Companion Bible; King James Version* (Grand Rapids: Kregel Publications, 1990), Appendix 6: Figures of Speech, 11.

19. John Murray, *The Imputation of Adam's Sin* (Phillipsburg, NJ: Presbyterian and Reformed Publishing Co., 1959), 33.

20. Jack S. Deere, "Deuteronomy" in *The Bible Knowledge Commentary; Old Testament* (Colorado Springs: ChariotVictor Publishing, 1985), 264-65.

21. Thomas R. Schreiner, *Adam, the Fall, and Original Sin*, 282.

22. John A. Witmer, "Romans," in The Bible Knowledge Commentary; New Testament (Colorado Springs, CO: ChariotVictor Publishing, 1983), 460.

23. Sir Robert Anderson, The Gospel And Its Ministry [London: James Nisbet & Co., 1886), 131.

24. John Nelson Darby, Darby's Synopsis of the Bible; Accessed August 28, 2018,

http://biblehub.com/commentaries/darby/romans/5.htm
25. Thomas R. Schreiner, Romans, (Grand Rapids: Baker Academic, 1998), 272.

Chapter III. Aurelius Augustine (354-430 A.D.)

In his book titled *In Adam's Fall* I.A. McFarland wrote that Augustine marked a *"transition from a loosely conceived, broadly ecumenial doctrine of the fall to a much more tightly formulated doctrine of original sin...Augustine's thought decisively redirected Christian interpretation of the fall."* [1]

1. Augustine's First Blunder

In regard to Augustine's interpretation of Romans 5:12 G. F. Wiggers wrote that *"The main scripture proof of original sin, Augustine found in the epistle to the Romans; and he must have found the more of it, the less he was an exegetical scholar and the less he knew of the original language of the New Testament. Romans 5:12, he used as the chief passage. He took it from the Latin translation. 'By one man, sin entered into the world, and death by sin, and so hath passed unto all men, in whom all have sinned...' In this he believed that he found the most complete proof for his original sin, propagating itself by generation."* [2]

Douglas J. Moo wrote that *"Augustine used Old Latin versions of the Greek New Testament in his interpretation of verse 12. He mistakenly read 'eph ho' as the Latin equivalent of 'in quo,' in whom. Augustine misrepresented the phrase to read, 'in whom all sinned.' He erroneously assumed that the relative pronoun had a pronominal force, with 'one man' serving as the antecedent. Augustine's mistranslation served as 'biblical support' for his influential doctrine of original sin."* [3]

Thomas Screiner wrote the following on the same subject:

"Romans 5:12-14. One of the most debated issues in the history of interpretation is the relationship between Adam's sin and the sins of his descendants. Augustine interpreted Romans 5:12 to say that 'in Adam' we all sinned. He based his interpretation on the Latin phrase 'in quo,' but the Greek wording is 'eph ho,' which is more plausibly rendered as 'on the basis of which.'" [4]

So we can see that Augustine made a huge error in regard to his main scripture proof of original sin. Next we will look at a passage which is about Adam's fall which Augustine also misinterpreted.

2. Eating of the Tree of the Knowledge of Good and Evil

We will see that Augustine's theory of Original Sin was also based on a misunderstanding of the following verses which speak of the results of Adam's eating of the Tree of the Knowledge of Good and Evil:

"And the LORD God said, **Behold, the man is become as one of us, to know good and evil: and now, lest he put forth his hand, and take also of the tree of life, and eat, and live for ever***: Therefore the LORD God sent him forth from the garden of Eden, to till the ground from whence he was taken. So he drove out the man; and he placed at the east of the garden of Eden Cherubims, and a flaming sword which turned every way, to keep the way of the tree of life"* (Gen.3:22-24).

First, we can understand that Adam was created in a mortal body because in order for him to live for ever it was necessary for him to eat of the Tree of Life. That idea is supported by by the *Cambridge Bible for Schools and Colleges*:

"Man must be prevented from eating of the Tree of Life, and so obtaining another prerogative of Divinity, that of immortality. **Man is created mortal**" [*emphasis added*]. [5]

Henry Alford wrote that "*man was created subject to death.*" [6]

Gerald Bray said that "**Adam was not created as an immortal being**, *but in the garden of Eden he was protected against death. When he fell the protection was removed and he suffered the consequences as his nature was allowed to take its course* " [*emphasis added*]. [7]

We also know that when Adam ate of that tree his physical body did not undergo a change in his physical makeup. Albert Barnes wrote the following:

"*The tree of the knowledge of good and evil effected a change, **not in the physical constitution of man**, but in his mental experience - in his knowledge of good and evil*" [*emphasis added*]. [8]

There is absolutely no evidence that the physical body of Adam was changed in any way at all. He died physically because he was denied the very thing which would have allowed him to live for ever--the Tree of Life. Despite this Augustine mistakenly believed that when Adam sinned he "despoiled his body":

G.F. Wiggers quoted Augustine saying the following: "*If Adam had not sinned, he would not have been despoiled of his body, but would have been clothed with immortality and incorruptibility, that what is mortal should be swallowed up of life...*" *De Pec. Mer. I. 2, 4.*" [*emphasis added*]. [9]

Again, David certainly did not believe that his body was corrupted in any way because he said the following:

"*For thou hast possessed my reins: thou hast covered me in my mother's womb. **I will praise thee; for I am fearfully and wonderfully made**: marvellous are thy works; and that my soul knoweth right well*" (Ps.139:13-14).

3. Augustine and the Change of the Body at the Fall

Wiggers says that "*Augustine explains himself to this effect, that **carnal concupiscence has its seat in the body** as well as in the soul. 'The cause of fleshly lust is not in the soul alone, and still much less in the body alone. For it arises from both; from the soul, because without it no delight is felt; **and from the flesh, because without this, no fleshly delight is felt,'** etc. X. 12.* " [emphasis added]. [10]

According to Augustine "the cause of fleshly lust" comes from both the body and the soul. However, the Lord Jesus said nothing about the physical body being its cause:

"*That which cometh out of the man, that defileth the man. **For from within, out of the heart of men, proceed evil thoughts, adulteries, fornications, murders**, Thefts, covetousness, wickedness, deceit, lasciviousness, an evil eye, blasphemy, pride, foolishness*" (Mk.7:20-22).

When the Lord Spoke of these things coming from "within" a man he was speaking of the inward man as opposed to the outward man of which Paul spoke:

"*For which cause we faint not; but though our **outward man** perish, yet the **inward man** is renewed day by day*" (2 Cor.4:16).

4. Did Adam's Body Acquired a Dying Nature?

According to Augustine as a result of Adam's sin the body acquired a sickly and dying nature:

"*Before the fall, and before there was any necessity of dying, concupiscence had no existence; but after **the body had acquired a sickly and dying nature**, (which likewise belongs to the flesh of animals), it received also, on this account, the movement by which **the carnal desire originates in animals**, whereby those that are born, succeed the dying.' De Gen. ad Lit. XI. 32*" [emphasis added]. [11]

The problem with Augustine's idea is that Adam was created with a mortal body because in order for him to live for ever it was necessary for him to partake of the Tree of Life. So when Adam ate of the forbidden tree his body did not take on a dying nature because he already had a mortal body.

5. Concupiscence

In order to understand the meaning of the word "concupiscence" let us look at this verse:

*"But sin, taking occasion by the commandment, wrought in me all manner of **concupiscence**"* (Ro.7:8).

The Greek word translated "concupiscence" means *"desire for what is forbidden, lust."* [12]

Wiggers says that Augustine called concupiscence "***a disease-- a wound inflicted on nature through the treacherous counsel given by the devil--a vice of nature--a deformity**--an evil that comes from the depravity of our nature which is vitiated by sin.' C. Jul. III. 15,26; V. 7. Op. Imp. IV. 33; V. 20. 'No man is now born without concupiscence.' I. 72."* [emphasis added]. [13]

According to Augustine this "concupiscence" is the punishment of sin and the guilt and the sign of sin:

"We are ashamed of that of which the first pair were ashamed when they covered their nakedness. This" (of which they were ashamed, concupiscence) *"is the punishment of sin, the guilt and the sign of sin, the inclination and the tinder to sin... De Nupt. et Conc. II. 9."* [14]

Augustine also believed that *"Original sin propagates itself by concupiscence...**sensual lust**, which is expiated only by the sacrament of regeneration, **propagates by generation the bond of sin to posterity**"* [emphasis added]. [15]

John Calvin followed Augustine in thinking that Adam's body

and his descendant's bodies are defiled as a result of concupisence, writing that "*everything which is in man, from the intellect to the will, **from the soul even to the flesh**, is defiled and pervaded with this concupiscence; or, to express it more briefly, that the whole man is in himself nothing else than concupiscence*" [emphasis added]. ⁱ⁶

The Westminster Confession of Faith follows Augustine by saying that Adam and Eve's corrupted nature was conveyed to their posterity by "ordinary generation":

"*They being the root of all mankind, the guilt of this sin was imputed; and the same death in sin, and corrupted nature, **conveyed to all their posterity descending from them by ordinary generation**" [emphasis added]. ⁱ⁷*

6. The Devil is the Corrupter of Our Substance

Augustine wrote that "'***The devil is the corrupter**, not the author **of our substance**. By that which he has inflicted, he subjects to himself what he did not create, a righteous God giving him this power; from whose power the devil withdraws neither himself nor what is subjected to him.' VI. 19.*" [emphasis added]. ⁱ⁸

Even today in Christendom there are some who speculate that the devil did indeed corrupt the body of Adam. Henri Blocher writes the following:

"*Ephesians 2 does conjoin the 'prince of aerial authority' with wrath-deserving 'nature.' In the story of Eden, in Genesis 3, the fall did mean 'leaving it to the snake'--yielding to the occult power 'who is called the Devil and Satan, who seduces the whole inhabited earth' (Rev.12:9). **I shall not enter here into the wide and disputed field of demonolgy and 'spiritual warfare', but shall 'cautiously' refer to some pastoral evidence of encroachment by evil spirits on human lineage; if confirmed, it*** *would strengthen the case of heredity in sinfulness*" [*emphasis added*]. [19]

In the same book Blocher asked, "***Dare I mention genetics? Even genetics should not be ruled out of court, since the dicipline deals with one level in the complex interaction of elements.*** *We should exclude the fantasy about a 'sin gene' or sin as a chromosomic aberration; this is far too crude, and a category error.* ***But could there be a far more subtle disorder of the genetic formula and its expression, a disorder which could correlate to spiritual deformation?*** *Might we imagine, for instance, that spiritual integrity could support protective or restorative mechanisms against detrimental mutations-- mechanisms which were lost?*" [*emphasis added*]. [20]

David Smith wrote that "*We may assume, then,* ***that each infant born into the world possesses that gene, as it were, that predisposes toward sin***" [*emphasis added*]. [21]

7. The Immaculate Conception of Mary

Gerald Bray writes that "*if sin is thought of as a congenital defect, an entirely different problem presents itself, which may be expressed as follows: 'If Jesus was a genuine human being and inherited his humanity from his mother, Mary, how was it that this humanity did not contain that defect? The only answer to this was to argue that at some point the defect had been removed from Mary. Most medieval theologians believed that this had occurred at the annunciation, when the archangel Gabriel declared that she was 'full of grace,' which they understood to mean that she had been cleansed from her sin before conceiving Jesus in her womb (Luke 1:28). Later on, under the pressure of popular piety as much as anything else. this idea was pushed to the point of saying that Mary herself was conceived and born without sin, presumably because her mother (and father?) had been cleansed before her conception.* **This is the doctrine of the so-called**

immaculate conception of the Blessed Virgin Mary, which since 1854 has been the official teaching of the Roman Catholic Church" [*emphasis added*]. [22]

Even this doesn't solve the problem for Rome because it doesn't answer the fact that the Lord Jesus was made like His brethren "in all things," the same teaching which is found in the following Bible approved by the church at Rome:

"*Wherefore it behoved him **in all things to be made like unto his brethren**, that he might become a merciful and faithful priest before God, that he might be a propitiation for the sins of the people*"(Heb.2:17; *Douay-Rheims Bible*).

Sir Robert Anderson wrote that "*the Roman Church was moulded by Augustine into the form it has ever since maintained. Of all the errors that later centuries developed in her teaching there is scarcely one that cannot be found in the embryo of his writings.*" [23]

End Notes

1. McFarland, *In Adam's Fall: A Meditation on the Christian Doctrine of Original Sin* (Malden, MA: Wiley-Blackwell, 2010), 32.

2. G. F. Wiggers, *Historical Presentation of Augustinism and Pelagianism From the Original Sources* (Andover: Gould, Newman & Saxton, 1840), 272.

3. *A Theology for the Church*, ed. Daniel Akin (Nashville, TN: B & H Publishing Group, 2014), 373-374.

4. Thomas R. Schreiner, *Paul: Apostle of God's Glory in Christ; A Pauline Theology* (Downer's Grove, IL: IVP Academic, 2001), 146.

5. *Cambridge Bible for Schools and Colleges*; Accessed August 1, 2017, http://biblehub.com/commentaries/cambridge/genesis/3.htm

6. Henry Alford, *The Book of Genesis and Part of the Book of Exodus; A Revised Edition* (London: John Childs and Son, 1872), 19.

7. Gerald Bray, "Sin in Historical Theology," in *Fallen: A Theology of Sin* ed. Christoper W. Morgan and Robert Peterson [Wheaton, IL: Crossway, 2013], 169.

8. Albert Barnes, *Barnes Notes on the Bible*, Accessed August 16, 2010, http://biblehub.com/commentaries/barnes/genesis/3.htm

9. G.F. Wiggers, *An Historical Presentation of Augustinism and Pelagianism From the Original Sources*, 92.

10. *Ibid.*, 95.

11. *Ibid.*

12. John Henry Thayer, *A Greek-English Lexicon of the New Testament*, 238.

13. G.F. Wiggers, *An Historical Presentation of Augustinism and Pelagianism From the Original Sources*, 95.

14. *Ibid.*, 93-94.

15. *Ibid.*, 89.

16. John Calvin, *Institutes of the Christian Religion*; 2:1:8.

17. *The Westminster Confession of Faith*; VI/3.

18. G.F. Wiggers, *An Historical Presentation of Augustinism and Pelagianism From the Original Sources*, 122.

19. Henry Blocher, *Original Sin: Illuminating the Riddle*, 126-127.

20. *Ibid.*, 124.

21. David L. Smith, *With Willful Intent. A Theology of Sin* (Weaton Bridgepoint, IL: Victor Books 1994), 369.

22. Gerald Bray, *Fallen: A Theology of Sin*, 170-71.

23. Sir Robert Anderson, *The Bible or the Church?* (London: Pickering and Inglis, Second Edition), 53.

Chapter IV. An Examination of the Natural Headship View of Original Sin

1. Augustine

C. F. Wiggers wrote that *"to the philosophic mind, Augustine also endeavored to make intelligible the possibility of the propagation of Adam's sin to his posterity; and this partly by allowing original sin to be propagated by concupiscence, **and partly by assuming, that we all existed in Adam, or as he also expressed himself, in allusion to Heb. 7:10, all were in the loins of Adam**"* [*emphasis added*]. [1]

Augustine's theory is dependent on the idea that all people were in Adam when he sinned and therefore when Adam sinned all people sinned in Adam. That idea is based on a literal reading of what is said about Levi in the following passage:

*"And as I may so say, Levi also, who receiveth tithes, payed tithes in Abraham. **For he was yet in the loins of his father**, when Melchisedec met him"* (Heb.7:9-10).

John Witmer writes that *"**The natural headship view...recognizes that the entire human race was seminally and 'physically' in Adam, the first man**. As a result God considered as participating in the act of sin which Adam committed and as receiving the penalty he received. Even adherents of the federal headship view must admit that Adam is the natural of the human race physically; the issue is the relationship spiritually. **Biblical evidence supports the natural headship of Adam. When presenting the superiority of Melchizedek's priesthood to Aaron's, the author of Hebrews argued that Levi, the head of the priestly tribe, 'who collects the 10th, paid the 10th through Abraham, because when Melchizedek met Abraham, Levi was* *still in the body of his ancestor' (Heb. 7:9-10)*" [*emphasis added*]. ²

The problem with this idea is the fact that people's "souls" do not come to people by ordinary generation and therefore they are not a part of anyone's "physical" make-up. There is no reason to suppose that Levi's "soul" was created at anytime prior to the time when he was conceived in the womb so it is clear that he was not in the loins of Abraham because his soul did not even exist when Abraham walked the earth. So even if it can be said that "*the entire human race was seminally and physically in Adam*" that idea fails to account for the fact that it is the LORD who makes people's souls when they are conceived and not before:

"**The spirit of God hath made me**, *and the breath of the Almighty hath given me life*" (Job.33:4).

"*But now, O LORD, thou art our father; we are the clay, and thou our potter; and* **we all are the work of thy hand**" (Isa.64:4).

"*Know ye that the LORD he is God:* **it is he that hath made us, and not we ourselves**; *we are his people, and the sheep of his pasture*" (Ps.100:3).

2. Literal or Non-Literal?

The question which must be asked is, "Can we take what is said in that Hebrews passage literally?" To answer that question let us look at that passage while paying particular attention to the part in "bold":

"*And here men that die receive tithes; but there he receiveth them, of whom it is witnessed that he liveth.* **And as I may so say**, *Levi also, who receiveth tithes, payed tithes in Abraham. For he was yet in the loins of his father, when Melchisedec met him*" (Heb.7:8-10).

Now let us read the comments of Albert Barnes on this verse:

> "***And as I may so say*** - *So to speak...For numerous examples in the classic writers of this expression, see Wetstein in loc. It is used precisely as it is with us when we say "so to speak," or 'if I may be allowed the expression.'* **It is employed when what is said is not strictly and literally true**, *but when it amounts to the same thing, or when about the same idea is conveyed. 'It is a 'softening down' of an expression which a writer supposes his readers may deem too strong, or which may have the appearance of excess or severity. It amounts to an indirect apology for employing an unusual or unexpected assertion or phrase.' 'Prof. Stuart.'* **Here Paul could not mean that Levi had actually paid tithes in Abraham - for he had not then an existence; or that Abraham was his representative - for there had been no appointment of Abraham to act in that capacity by Levi; or that the act of Abraham was imputed or reckoned to Levi, for that was not true, and would not have been pertinent to the case if it were so**" [*emphasis added*]. [3]

Of course what the author said at Hebrews 7:9-10 cannot be taken literally. The author of Hebrews was merely using a figure of speech in order to assert that Melchisedec's priesthood was superior to the Levitical priesthood. That explains why the author used the opening words "And as I may so say. " According to A. R. Fausset that phrase can only be understood in a figurative sense: "*as I may so say-**to preclude what he is about to say being taken in the mere literal sense***" [*emphasis added*]. [4]

The argument used by the proponents of the theory of Original Sin that all people sin in Adam and with Adam falls completely apart when we realize that what is said at Hebrews 7:9-10 cannot be taken literally. There is absolutely no Scriptual evidence to support either the Natural Headship Theory or the Federal Headship Theory.

S. Lewis Johnson does not agree with the "natural headship" theory, saying that those who do "*have sought to teach that just as Levi was in Abraham when Abraham paid tithes, so we were in Adam really, and when Adam sinned, we acted. Now, that's nonsense. They speak of seminal relationship. They speak of a natural headship. I believe that Adam was our natural head, as well as our representative head. But the analogy is broken.* ***If it were true that by the one act of Adam we were plunged into death because we acted then, Paul draws an analogy with the sacrifice of Jesus Christ gaining us salvation. Is it true that I was in Christ and I performed the act of the cross? No. No one who held that view would say that.*** *But Paul draws this analogy. With Paul, you see, it is a legal thing. It is a representative thing. It is one man who acts as our representative and plunges us into sin"* [emphasis added]. [5]

3. The Natural Headship View and Romans 5:12d

Douglas Moo says that the sin attributed to "all" in the following verse in "bold" is identical to the sin committed by Adam:

"*For this cause, even as by one man sin entered into the world, and by sin death; and thus death passed upon all men,* ***for that all have sinned***" (Ro.5:12; DBY).

He writes that "*If we are to read verse 12d in light of verses 18-19, 'all sinned' must be given some kind of 'corporate' meaning: 'sinning' not as voluntary acts of sin in 'one's own person,' but sinning 'in and with' Adam....****The point is rather that the sin attributed to the 'all' is to be understood, in the light of verses 12a-c and 15-19, as a sin that in some manner is identical to the sin committed by Adam***. *Paul can therefore say both 'all die because all sin' and 'all die because Adam sinned' with no hint of conflict, because* ***the sin of Adam 'is' the sin of all***. *All people, therefore, stand condemned 'in Adam,' guilty by reason of the sin committed 'in him.' This interpretation is defended by a great number of exegetes and theologians*" [emphasis added]. [6]

Moo teaches that the sin of Adam 'is' the sin of all. However,

Paul makes it clear that the sins of those who lived between Adam and Moses was not the same sin committed by Adam:

"For this cause, even as by one man sin entered into the world, and by sin death; and thus death passed upon all men, for that all have sinned: for until law sin was in the world; but sin is not put to account when there is no law; **but death reigned from Adam until Moses, even upon those who had not sinned in the likeness of Adam's transgression**" (Ro.5:12-15; DBY).

Schreiner also sees this same truth, writing that "*Paul specifically and emphatically distinguishes the sin of those who live in the era between Adam and Moses from Adam's sin.*" [7]

Schreiner correctly points out that "*Those who lived in the era between Adam and Moses were accountable for their sin, so that they were condemned because they violated God's moral norms. Their sin was counted against them and thus they were judged. Paul himself teaches the same truth in 2:12, when he claims that 'all those who sinned without the law will also perish without the law'...What Paul claims here fits with the judgments inflicted on the flood generation and at Babel.* **Gentiles did not have the Mosaic law, but they were judged for violating the unwritten law--the law inscribed on their hearts**. *Romans 2:12 is of paramount importance, for it prevents us from adopting a mistaken view of 5:12-14.*" [8]

4. The Natural Headship View and the "One" Sin of Adam

Murray points out another problem with the Natural Headship Theory:

"*It may not be questioned that there is something severely unique and distinct about our involvement in the sin of Adam. The sin is the 'one' sin of Adam. If the relationship to Adam were simply that of seminal union, that of being in his loins, that would not provide any explanation why the sin imputed is the first sin 'alone.' We were as much in his loins when he committed other sins and these other sins would be just as applicable to us as his first sin if the whole explanation of the imputation of his first sin resides in the fact that we were in his loins. Hence some additional factor is required to explain the restriction to the one sin of Adam."* [9]

It is a fact that my interpretation of Romans 5:12-21 reveals that it was the "one" sin of Adam, the eating of the Tree of the Knowledge of Good and Evil, which resulted in the spiritual death of all people who sin. When Adam ate of the forbidden tree he received a "conscience" of the law written in the heart and after that all of his posterity likewise received a conscience when they were made in the image of Adam. Then spiritual death came upon all men when they sinned against their conscience. That explains why Paul stresses that it was just the "one" sin of Adam which resulted in the spiritual death of all people when they sin.

End Notes

1. C.F. Wiggers, *An Historical Presentation of Augustinism and Pelagianism From the Original Sources*, 278.

2. John A. Witmer, " Romans," in *The Bible Knowledge Commentary; New Testament*, 458.

3. Albert Barnes, *Notes, Explanatory and Practical, on the Epistle to the Hebrews* (New York: Harper & Brothers, 1855), 159.

4. Robert Jamieson, A. R. Fausset and David Brown, *Commentary Critical and Explanatory on the Whole Bible*; Accessed August 17, 2018, https://www.blueletterbible.org/Comm/jfb/Hbr/Hbr_007.cfm?a=1140010.

5. S. Lewis Johnson, *The Imputation of Adam's Sin of His Posterity*; Accessed August 17, 2008, http://sljinstitute.net/three-great-imputations/the-imputation-of-adams-sin-of-his-posterity/

6. Douglas J. Moo, *Fallen: A Theology of Sin*, 124.

7. Thomas R. Schreiner, *Adam, the Fall, and Original Sin*, 287.

8. *Ibid.*, 279-80.

9. John Murray, *The Imputation of Adam's Sin*, 38-39.

Chapter V. An Examination of the Federal Headship View of Original Sin

John Witmer writes that "*The federal headship view considers Adam, the first man, as the **'representative' of the human race** that generated from him. As the representative of all humans, Adam's act of sin was considered by God to be the act of all people and **his penalty of death was judically made the penalty of everybody**"* [emphasis added]. [1]

According to the Federal Headship View Adam is the federal head of the "covenant" spoken of in the *Westminster Larger Catechism*:

"*The providence of God toward man in the estate in which he was created, was the placing him in paradise, appointing him to dress it, giving him liberty to eat of the fruit of the earth; putting the creatures under his dominion, and ordaining marriage for his help; affording him communion with himself; instituting the sabbath; **entering into a covenant of life with him**, upon condition of personal, perfect, and perpetual obedience, of which the tree of life was a pledge; and forbidding to eat of the tree of knowledge of good and evil, upon the pain of death*" [emphasis added]. [2]

According to the same Catechism when Adam sinned his posterity sinned in him and fell with him:

"*The covenant being made with Adam as a public person, not for himself only, but for his posterity, all mankind descending from him by ordinary generation, sinned in him, and fell with him in that first transgression.*" [3]

Then we read that Adam's sin was conveyed unto his posterity by natural generation and "in that way" all people are conceived and born in sin:

"Original sin is conveyed from our first parents unto their posterity by natural generation, so as all that proceed from them in that way are conceived and born in sin." [4]

The problem with this view is that when a person is conceived by natural generation only his physical body comes into existence in that way and not his soul, which is made by the LORD. And it has already been shown that David believed that his body was "wonderfully made." There is not any evidence that anyone's physical body emerges from the womb with defects due to Adam's sin. Therefore, it is impossible that anyone is either conceived in sin or born in sin by natural generation.

1. The Son Shall Not Bear the Iniquity of the Father

The Scriptures indicate that the penalty of a person's sin will not be made the penalty for that person's descendants. Let us look at what is said here:

"The word of the LORD came unto me again, saying, What mean ye, that ye use this proverb concerning the land of Israel, saying, The fathers have eaten sour grapes, and the children's teeth are set on edge?" (Ezek.18:1-2).

Charles Dyer wrote that "*God asked Ezekiel about a **proverb** being circulated. This proverb--**The Fathers eat sour grapes, and the children's teeth are set on edge**--must have been well known in Israel because Jeremiah also quoted it (cf. Jer. 31:29-30). The proverb's point was that children were suffering because of their parents' sins...So these people were blaming God for punishing them unjustly (cf. Ezek. 18:25). God saw that this **proverb** had to be refuted...Blaming others for their misfortunes, the people were denying their own guilt. This was wrong because every individual is personally responsible to God...Those who are guilty will receive their own deserved punishment.*" [5]

Later we read the LORD's conclusion about this matter:

"*The soul that sinneth, it shall die. **The son shall not bear the iniquity of the father**, neither shall the father bear the iniquity of the son*" (Ezek.18:20).

There are many places in the Bible where this truth is revealed:

"*The fathers shall not be put to death for the children, **neither shall the children be put to death for the fathers: every man shall be put to death for his own sin***" (Deut.24:16).

"*But he slew not their children, but did as it is written in the law in the book of Moses, where the LORD commanded, saying, The fathers shall not die for the children, **neither shall the children die for the fathers, but every man shall die for his own sin***" (2 Chron.25:4).

Despite this evidence that the son will not bear the iniquity of the father those who promote the theory of Original Sin teach that the LORD did that very thing when He imputed the guilt of Adam's sin to all of his offspring. According to the Federal Headship theory Adam's sin was considered by the LORD to be the sin of all of his offspring.

2. In Adam All Die: 1 Corinthians 15:22

John Murray, who supports the Federal Headship view, writes that "*In 1 Corinthians 2:22, 45-49 Paul provides us with what is one of the most striking and significant rubics in all of Scripture. He comprehends God's dealings with men under **the twofold headships of two Adams**...Adam and Christ sustain unique relations to men. And that history and destiny are determined by these relationships is demonstrated by verse 22: 'As in Adam all die, even so in Christ all shall be made alive'...**the kind of relationship which Adam sustains to men is after the pattern of the realationship which Christ sustains to men**" [*emphasis added*]. [6]

57

Yes, the pattern of the relationship which Christ sustains to men is after the pattern of the relationship which Adam sustains to men. And since no one is automatically "in Christ" then the same must be true for those "in Adam." No one is "in Christ" until they do something, and that thing is to believe. And no one is "in Adam" until they sin.

Therefore, we can understand that no one can be under the "headship of Christ" until they believe just like no one can be considered under the "headship of Adam" until they sin.

In his comments on this verse Albert Barnes wrote that " *if this passage means, that in Adam, or by him, all people became sinners, then the correspondent declaration 'all shall be made alive' must mean that all people shall become righteous, or that all shall be saved. This would be the natural and obvious interpretation; since the words 'be made alive' must have reference to the words 'all die,' and must affirm the co-relative and opposite fact.* **If the phrase 'all die' there means all become sinners, then the phrase 'all be made alive' must mean all shall be made holy, or be recovered from their spiritual death; and thus an obvious argument is furnished for the doctrine of universal salvation**, *which it is difficult, if not impossible, to meet. It is not a sufficient answer to this to say, that the word 'all,' in the latter part of the sentence, means all the elect, or all the righteous; for its most natural and obvious meaning is, that it is co-extensive with the word 'all' in the former part of the verse*" [*emphasis added*]. ⁷

3. The Representative View Makes No Sense

From the Scriptures we know that the LORD God loves the world (Jn.3:16) and that He doesn't want anyone to perish (2 Pet.3:9) and He wants all men to be saved:

"*For this is good and acceptable in the sight of God our*

Saviour; ***Who will have all men to be saved, and to come unto the knowledge of the truth***" (1 Tim.2:3-4).

However, if the theory of Original Sin is correct then the LORD set up a system which practically guarantees that no one will be saved because no one will come to the truth. According to the Federal Headship theory Adam was mankind's representative by divine appointment. And once he sinned, his corrupted nature as well as the guilt of his sin was conveyed to all of his posterity. As a result, all people emerge from the womb "*made opposite unto all that is spiritually good, and wholly inclined to all evil.*" [8]

The LORD had already dealt with Lucifer who had a free will so He certainly knew the perils associated with His creatures having free will. And even with that knowledge, according to the theory of Original Sin, the LORD set up a system whereby if Adam exercised his free will and ate of the tree of the knowledge of good and evil then all people emerge from the womb wholly inclined to all evil. If the LORD actually set up such a system then practically no one will come to the light of the gospel according to what is written here:

"*For God sent not his Son into the world to condemn the world; but that the world through him might be saved. He that believeth on him is not condemned: but he that believeth not is condemned already, because he hath not believed in the name of the only begotten Son of God.* **And this is the condemnation, that light is come into the world, and men loved darkness rather than light, because their deeds were evil. For every one that doeth evil hateth the light, neither cometh to the light**, *lest his deeds should be reproved. But he that doeth truth cometh to the light, that his deeds may be made manifest, that they are wrought in God*" (Jn.3:17-21).

According to the theory of Original Sin the LORD set up a system and according to that system when Adam sinned then as a result all people emerge from the womb wholly inclined to all evil. And because of their evil deeds they hate the word of God and do not believe it either. It makes absolutely no sense that the

Lord would set up such a system because that system practically ensures that no one will believe and that all will perish even though the LORD does not want any to perish.

End Notes

1. John A. Witmer, *The Bible Knowledge Commentary; New Testament*, 458.

2. *Westminster Larger Catechism*, "Answer to Question #20", (CRTA); Accessed July 27, 2018, http://reformed.org/documents/wlc_w_proofs/index.html

3. *Ibid.*, "Answer to Question #22."

4. *Ibid.*, "Answer to Question #26."

5. Charles H. Dyer, "Ezekiel," in *The Bible Knowledge Commentary; Old Testament*, 1260.

6. John Murray, *The Imputation of Adam's Sin*, (Phillipsburg, NJ: Presbyterian and Reformed Publishing Co., 1959), 39.

7. Albert Barnes, *Notes on the Bible*; Accessed July 15, 2018, http://biblehub.com/commentaries/barnes/1_corinthians/15.htm

8. *Westminster Larger Catechism*, "Answer to Question #25."

Chapter VI: Original Sin is an Offense to Human Reason

The Barna Research Group did a Survey of Christians in 2002 and this is what the found about their belief in the theory of Original Sin:

"In yet another break from biblical teaching, **three-quarters of adults (74%) agree that, 'when people are born they are neither good nor evil - they make a choice between the two as they mature.'** *In other words, the concept of original sin is rejected by most Americans in favor of a rational choice approach to human nature. At least seven out of ten members of every demographic segment examined accepts the notion of choice over that of original sin. Unexpectedly, the survey data reveal that a slight majority of evangelicals (52%) also buy this notion"* [emphasis added]. [1]

It is not difficult to understand why most American Christians reject the theory. John Stuart Mill wrote that *"the rational attitude of a thinking mind towards the supernatural, whether in natural or in revealed religion, is that of scepticism."* [2]

All people have a conscience which reveals what is right and wrong in the LORD's eyes and it serves as a moral compass. All people know instinctively that a person cannot be judged guilty for someone else's sin. In fact, the Scriptures reveal that the ability to reason between what is right and wrong is what separates those who are "babes" in Christ from those who are "full age":

"For every one that useth milk is unskilful in the word of righteousness: for he is a babe. But strong meat belongeth to them that are of full age, **even those who by reason of use have their senses exercised to discern both good and evil**" (Heb.5:13-14).

Even those who actually defend the theory of Original Sin admit that it defies human reason, as witnessed by the following words of Thomas Schreiner:

"*The doctrine of original sin is not irrational, but **it is an offense to human reason**" [emphasis added].* [3]

Pope Benedict XVI calls the theory "illogical":

"*Evil is not logical. Only God and good are logical, are light. Evil remains mysterious. **It is presented as such in great images, as it is in chapter 3 of Genesis, with that scene of the two trees, of the serpent, of sinful man: a great image that makes us guess but cannot explain what is itself illogical.** We may guess, not explain; nor may we recount it as one fact beside another, because it is a deeper reality. It remains a mystery of darkness, of night*" [emphasis added]. [4]

Blaise Paschal, another advocate of the theory, says the following:

"***Original sin is folly in the eyes of men**, but it is put forward as such. You should therefore not reproach me for **the unreasonable nature of this doctrine**, because I put it forward as being unreasonable. But this folly is wiser than all men's wisdom, it is wiser than men. For without it, what are we to say man is? His whole state depends on this imperceptible point. How could he have become aware of it through his reason seeing that **it is something contrary to reason**, and that his reason far from discovering it by its own methods draws away when faced with it?*" [emphasis added]. [5]

Why should anyone have to throw their reason to the wind in order to accept the theory of Original Sin because, according to Paul, truth comes from reasoning out of the Scriptures?:

"*And Paul, as his manner was, went in unto them, and three sabbath days **reasoned with them out of the scriptures**"* (Acts 17:2).

Since most Christians reject the theory which is taught as fact in most churches then imagine what the unsaved think of it. The theory is met with an even greater degree of scepticism with them. According to the theory of Original Sin every person enters the world "*made opposite to all good, and wholly inclined to all evil.*" [6]

According to the theory the LORD makes people wholly inclined to all evil and then he punishes them for doing the very thing which He designed them to do:

"*But after thy hardness and impenitent heart treasurest up unto thyself wrath against the day of wrath and revelation of the righteous judgment of God;* **Who will render to every man according to his deeds**: *To them who by patient continuance in well doing seek for glory and honour and immortality, eternal life: But unto them that are contentious, and do not obey the truth, but obey unrighteousness, indignation and wrath,* **Tribulation and anguish, upon every soul of man that doeth evil**, *of the Jew first, and also of the Gentile*" (Ro.2:5-9).

Sir Robert Anderson writes, "*As the Westminster Divines express it, 'We are utterly indisposed, disabled, and made opposite to all good.' This theology obviously impugns the righteousness of God in punishing men for their sins. In fact, it represents Him as a tyrant who punishes the lame for limping and the blind for losing their way.*" [7]

The Scriptures also reveal that the LORD is our Potter and we are the work of His hand:

"*But now, O LORD, thou art our father; we are the clay, and thou our potter; and we all are the work of thy hand*" (Isa.64:8).

The theory of Original Sin portrays the LORD as a mad Potter who makes His vessels with the express purpose of destroying some of them!

In Ayn Rand's book *For the New Intellectal* we read the following speech of Jon Gault where he critiques the teaching of Original Sin:

"Your code begins by damning man as evil, then demands that he practice a good which it defines as impossible for him to practice. It demands, as his first proof of virtue, that he accept his own depravity without proof. It demands that he start, not with a standard of value, but with a standard of evil, which is himself, by means of which he is then to define the good: the good is that which he is not.

"It does not matter who then becomes the profiteer on his renounced glory and tormented soul, a mystic God with some incomprehensible design or any passer-by whose rotting sores are held as some inexplicable claim upon him--it does not matter, the good is not for him to understand, his duty is to crawl through years of penance, atoning for the guilt of his existence to any stray collector of unintelligible debts, his only concept of a value is a zero: the good is that which is non-man.

"The name of this monstrous absurdity is Original Sin.

"A sin without volition is a slap at morality and an insolent contradiction in terms: that which is outside the possibility of choice is outside the province of morality. If man is evil by birth, he has no will, no power to change it; if he has no will, he can be neither good nor evil; a robot is amoral. To hold, as man's sin, a fact not open to his choice is a mockery of morality. To hold man's nature as his sin is a mockery of nature. To punish him for a crime he committed before he was born is a mockery of justice. To hold him guilty in a matter where no innocence exists is a mockery of reason. To destroy morality, nature, justice and reason by means of a single concept is a feat of evil hardly to be matched. Yet that is the root of your code.

"Do not hide behind the cowardly evasion that man is born with free will, but with a 'tendency' to evil. A free will saddled with a tendency is like a game with loaded dice. It forces man to struggle through the effort of playing, to bear responsibility and pay for the game, but the decision is weighted in favor of a tendency that he had no power to escape. If the tendency is of his choice, he cannot possess it at birth; if it is not of his choice, his *will is not free.*

"What is the nature of the guilt that your teachers call his Original Sin? What are the evils man acquired when he fell from a state they consider perfection? Their myth declares that he ate the fruit of the tree of knowledge--he acquired a mind and became a rational being. It was the knowledge of good and evil--he became a moral being. He was sentenced to earn his bread by his labor--he became a productive being. He was sentenced to experience desire--he acquired the capacity of sexual enjoyment. The evils for which they damn him are reason, morality, creativeness, joy--all the cardinal values of his existence. It is not his vices that their myth of man's fall is designed to explain and condemn, it is not his errors that they hold as his guilt, but the essence of his nature as man. Whatever he was--that robot in the Garden of Eden, who existed without mind, without values, without labor, without love--he was not man.

"Man's fall, according to your teachers, was that he gained the virtues required to live. These virtues, by their standard, are his Sin. His evil, they charge, is that he's man. His guilt, they charge, is that he lives.

"They call it a morality of mercy and a doctrine of love for man." [8]

End Notes

1. Barna Research Group, *Americans Draw Theological Beliefs From Different Points of View*; Accessed August 3, 2018, https://www.barna.com/research/americans-draw-theological-beliefs-from-diverse-points-of-view/

2. John Stuart Mill, *Essays on Ethics, Religion, and Society* [Toronto: University of Toronto Press, 1969], 482.

3. Thomas R. Schreiner, *Adam, the Fall, and Original Sin*, 287.

4. Pope Benedict XVI, *The Apostle's teaching on the relation between Adam and Christ*; Accessed August 5, 2018, https://www.catholicculture.org/culture/library/view.cfm?recnum=8580

5. Blaise Pascal, *Pensees*, (New York: Penguin, 1966), 695/445.

6. *Westminster Confession of Faith*; VI/4.

7. Sir Robert Anderson, *Misundersood Texts of the New Testament* (Grand Rapids: Kregel, 1991), 75.

8. Ayn Rand, *For the New Intellectual*, Accessed November 6, 2016, http://aynrandlexicon.com/lexicon/original_sin.html.

Chapter VII: Conclusion

To the Praise of His Glorious Grace

One of the LORD's purposes for the Christians He has called out of darkness is that they should praise Him as well as His glorious grace:

"*But you are a chosen people, a royal priesthood, a holy nation, God's special possession,* **that you may declare the praises of him who called you out of darkness into his wonderful light**" (1 Pet.2:9; NIV).

"**To the praise of his glorious grace**, *which he has freely given us in the One he loves. In him we have redemption through his blood, the forgiveness of sins,* **in accordance with the riches of God's grace that he lavished on us**" (Eph.1:6-8).

In the following passage Sir Robert Anderson speaks of the LORD's grace, writing that "*if grace be on the throne, what limits can be set to it? If that sin committed upon Calvary has not shut the door of mercy, all other sins together shall not avail to close it. If God can bless in spite of the death of Christ, who may not be blest? Innocence lost, conscience disobeyed and stifled, covenants and promises despised and forfeited, law trampled under foot, prophets persecuted, and last and unutterably terrible, the Only-begotten slain. And yet there is mercy still! What a gospel that would be!*

"*But 'the gospel of the glory of the blessed God' is something infinitely higher still. It is not that Calvary has failed to quench the love of God to men, but that it is the proof and measure of that love. Not that the death of Christ has failed to shut heaven against the sinner, but that heaven is open to the sinner by virtue of that death. The everlasting doors that lifted up their heads for Him are open for the guiltiest of men, and the blood by which the Lord of glory entered there is their title to approach. The way to heaven is as free as the way to hell. In hell there is an accuser, but in heaven there is no one to condemn. The only being in the universe of God who has a right to judge the sinner is now exalted to be a Saviour. Amid the wonders and terrors of that throne, He is a Saviour, and He is sitting there in grace."* [1]

The Apostle Paul warned those who received his epistles that there would be people in the local churches who would pervert the Scriptures:

"For I know this, that after my departing shall grievous wolves enter in among you, not sparing the flock. Also of your own selves shall men arise, speaking perverse things, to draw away disciples after them. Therefore watch, and remember, that by the space of three years I ceased not to warn every one night and day with tears" (Acts 20:29-31).

Paul also identified some of the "grievous wolves" who would pervert the Scriptures:

"And no marvel; for Satan himself is transformed into an angel of light. Therefore it is no great thing if his ministers also be transformed as the ministers of righteousness; whose end shall be according to their works" (2 Cor.11:14-15).

In the following passage Paul reveals the method that Satan and his ministers employ in order to pervert the glorious gospel of the grace of God:

"And even if our gospel is veiled, it is veiled to those who are perishing. **The god of this age has blinded the minds of unbelievers, so that they cannot see the light of the gospel that displays the glory of Christ**, *who is the image of God"* (2 Cor.4:3-5; NIV).

One of the ways that Satan and his minions blind the minds of people to the light of the gospel of the grace of God is by presenting the LORD as a God who is not gracious and will

69

impute the sin of Adam to everyone, including infants. Anderson writes the following about what he calls the "*gross and profane misrepresentation of God*" which "*is an essential part of the historic religion of Christendom*":

"HERE *is an infant, born but yesterday, and yet so frail and sickly that its young life may flicker out at any moment. The question arises, If it should die, what is to be its future? If it dies in its present condition, we are told it must be lost, heaven it cannot enter. But, we plead, the poor creature does not know its right hand from its left; it is absolutely innocent. Why should it be thus punished? Personally innocent, yes, we are answered; but by natural generation it belongs to the fallen race, and Adam's sin must banish it to hell, unless by regeneration it is brought within the family of God. But by the sacrament of baptism this change can be brought about without delay or difficulty, and thus the child's salvation can be secured if death should seize on it. Any one, perhaps, can perform the rite; but, as that is a disputed point, it may be well to make assurance still more sure, and call in the aid of one who is divinely appointed to administer the sacraments. But suppose the man we summon to our aid should be false to his profession, and prove to be of evil character and immoral life?*

"*That, we are assured, will in no way affect the validity of the sacrament, or the reality of the change which it will produce in the child. If the man be lawfully ordained, God will acknowledge him as His minister, notwithstanding.*

"*In a case of this kind nothing is gained by an appeal to passion. But will thoughtful and fair minds consider the matter, and honestly answer the question, whether even in the superstitions of Pagan races to whom we send out missionaries, there can be found a conception of God more unworthy, more revolting than this.*

"*What kind of God is this that is thus presented to us? A Being, unjust, unloving, and cruel, who devotes an innocent and helpless infant to destruction. A Being, unreasonable, arbitrary, and capricious, who will change its eternal destiny if a few drops of water are sprinkled upon it, accompanied by the utterance of a few cabalistic words. An unholy, an immoral Being, for He employs and recognises agents no matter what their character and life may be."* ²

Edward Bouverie Pusey wrote that "*The Bible is God's Word, and through it God the Holy Ghost, who spake it, speaks to the soul which closes not itself against it.*" ³

It is impossible to know just how many earnest seekers of the truth of God closed their minds to Christianity upon hearing what is taught within Christendom about Original Sin but the number must be enormous--perhaps in the millions. Besides that, how many people in the future will not come to the light of the glorious gospel because they first heard the teaching of Original Sin? That number can also be an enormous number. Even today the Jews say that Paul taught Original Sin and quote the following passage in an effort to persuade others not to follow his teachings:

"*If thou shalt hearken unto the voice of the LORD thy God, to keep his commandments and his statutes which are written in this book of the law, and if thou turn unto the LORD thy God with all thine heart, and with all thy soul. For this commandment which I command thee this day, it is not hidden from thee, neither is it far off. It is not in heaven, that thou shouldest say, Who shall go up for us to heaven, and bring it unto us, that we may hear it, and do it? Neither is it beyond the sea, that thou shouldest say, Who shall go over the sea for us, and bring it unto us, that we may hear it, and do it? But the word is very nigh unto thee, in thy mouth, and in thy heart, **that thou may do it**"* (Deut.30:10-14).

Rabbi Tovia Singer asks, "*How could the authors of the New Testament reasonably insist that man's dire condition was hopeless if the Torah unambiguously declared that man possessed an extraordinary ability to remain faithful to God?...Employing unparalleled literary manipulation, however, Paul manages to conceal this vexing theological problem with a swipe of his well-worn eraser. In fact, Paul's innovative approach to biblical tampering was so stunning that it would set the standard of scriptural revisionism for future New Testament authors.*

"A classic example of this biblical revisionism can be found in Romans 10:8 where Paul proclaims that he is quoting directly from Scripture as he records the words of Deuteronomy 30:14. Yet as he approaches the last portion of this verse, he carefully stops short of the Torah's vital conclusion and expunges the remaining segment of this crucial verse. In Romans Paul writes, 'But what does it say? 'The word is near you, in your mouth and in your heart (that is, the word of faith which we preach)' (Romans 10:8)."

Singer continues, writing that *"Predictably, the last words of Deuteronomy 30:14, 'that you may do it,' were meticulously deleted by Paul. Bear in mind that he had good reason for removing this clause - the powerful message conveyed in these closing words rendered all that Paul was preaching as heresy."* [4]

Besides that, R.C. Sproul teaches that the LORD is "punishing" all of mankind for Adam's sin:

"The doctrine of original sin does not refer to the first sin committed by Adam and Eve, but to the 'result' of that first sin. **Original sin is the corruption visited on the progeny of our first parents as punishment for the original transgression**" [*emphasis added*]. [5]

Then to top it off Calvin declared that the LORD arranged it "at his own pleasure":

"God not only foresaw the fall of the first man, and in him the ruin of his posterity **but also at his own pleasure arranged it**" [*emphasis added*]. [6]

For almost 1500 years the church at Rome held captive the truth of salvation by grace through faith alone but that changed beginning with Martin Luther. However, the theory of Original Sin continues to be preached in Protestant pulpits even though the Reformers declared that "*the visible Church of Christ is a congregation of faithful men in which the pure word of God is preached."* If anyone is preaching Original Sin then he is not preaching the pure word of God. Paul tells us how we are to confront false teaching:

"Put on the whole armour of God, that ye may be able to stand against the wiles of the devil. For we wrestle not against flesh and blood, but against principalities, against powers, against the rulers of the darkness of this world, against spiritual wickedness in high places. Wherefore take unto you the whole armour of God, that ye may be able to withstand in the evil day, and having done all, to stand. Stand therefore, having your loins girt about with truth, and having on the breastplate of righteousness; And your feet shod with the preparation of the gospel of peace; Above all, taking the shield of faith, wherewith ye shall be able to quench all the fiery darts of the wicked. And take the helmet of salvation, and the sword of the Spirit, which is the word of God" (Eph.6:11-17).

Christians have the sword of the Spirit, which is the word of God, not only to stand against Satan but also to completely destroy the false theory of Original Sin. Now it is up to Christians to band together and scream from the rooftops a denial of this false theory which darkens the character of the LORD God. Let us all begin to sing a new song, absent the theory of Original Sin:

"He brought me up also out of an horrible pit, out of the miry clay, and set my feet upon a rock, and established my goings. And he hath put a new song in my mouth, even praise unto our God: many shall see it, and fear, and shall trust in the LORD" (Ps.40:2-3).

End Notes

1. Sir Robert Anderson, *The Gospel and Its Ministry* (London: James Nisbet & Co., 1886), 16-17.
2. Sir Robert Anderson, *The Bible or the Church?*, 110-111.
3. Edward Bouverie Pusey, *Daniel the Prophet: Nine Lectures* (London: James Parker & Co., Oxford, 1868), Preface, xxv.
4. Rabbi Tovia Singer, "Does Judaism Believe in Original Sin?" *Outreach Judaism*; Accessed September 16, 2018, https://outreachjudaism.org/original-sin/
5. R. C. Sproul, *What is Reformed Theology?* 121.
6. John Calvin, *Institutes of the Christian Religion*, Book III, Chapter 23, Section 7.

Appendix #1: "Born of Water and the Spirit"

One of the better known interpretive problems facing Christians is found in the Nicodemus sermon, where the Lord Jesus declared, "unless one is born of water and the Spirit he cannot enter into the kingdom of God" (Jn.3:5). Some people teach that this is referring to water baptism and others say that it is referring to two baptisms, one with water and the other with the Spirit. In fact, there seems to be no concensus within Christianity concerning its meaning despite the fact that strong opinions are held on all sides. However, any misinterpretation of these words can lead to confusion in regard to the the doctrine of new birth.

The Solution Proposed by Sir Robert Anderson

In regard to the meaning of "water" at John 3:5 Anderson quotes the following verse which is also in reference to the new birth and calls attention to the Greek word *loutron,* which is translated as "washing":

"*He saved us, not on the basis of deeds which we have done in righteousness, but according to His mercy, by the **washing (loutron) of regeneration** and renewing by the Holy Spirit*" (Titus 5:5).

The following translation from the *New International Version* of the Bible uses the word "rebirth" instead of "regeneration," leaving no doubt that the new birth of John 3:3-5 is in view:

"*he saved us, not because of righteous things we had done, but because of his mercy. He saved us through the **washing (loutron) of rebirth** and renewal by the Holy Spirit*" (Titus 3:5; NIV).

The Touching of a Dead Body

In regard to the Greek word *loutron* Sir Robert writes that "*the LXX uses it twice; namely in Cant. iv.2 (where it is the washing place for sheep); and in Ecclesiasticus xxxiv. 25 where the Son of Sairach writes: 'He that washeth himself after the touching of a dead body, if he touch it again what avails his loutron?'*" [1]

Anderson continues, writing that "*This last passage is of the very highest importance here, and gives us the clew we are in search of. The reference is to one of the principal ordinances of the Mosaic ritual--a type, moreover, which fills a large place in New Testament doctrine--especially in Hebrews--namely the great sin-offering with the 'water of purification' (Num. xix.).*" [2]

At Ecclesiasticus 34:25 the reference to " touching a corpse" and "water" is in regard to the sin-offering of the red heifer spoken of here:

"*'The one who touches the corpse of any person shall be unclean for seven days. That one shall purify himself from uncleanness with the water on the third day and on the seventh day, and then he will be clean....*" (Num.19:11-12).

A red heifer, which was a sin-offering, was slaughtered by a priest and the ashes were gathered up and placed in a clean place. This sin-offering is a type of the Lord Jesus's death and Alda R. Habershon writes that "*The ashes speak of the finished work; for they show that the sacrifice has been accepted.*" [3] Then water was poured over the ashes and as a result the water served as a purification from sin:

"*'Now a man who is clean shall gather up the ashes of the heifer and deposit them outside the camp in a clean place, and the congregation of the sons of Israel shall keep it as water to remove impurity; it is purification from sin*" (Num.19:9).

The Loutron

Anderson says, "*The word rendered 'washing' is a noun, not a verb. This loutron is, strictly speaking, not the washing, but the vessel which contains the water.*" [4]

The Greek word *loutron* comes from the word *louo* and the suffix *tron*. The word *louo* means "*to bathe, wash.*" The suffix *tron* is a Greek suffix denoting an "*intrument.*" One of the meanings of the word "instrument" is "*utensil, container.*"

Therefore, the Greek word *loutron* can carry with it the meaning of a vessel containing water that has flowed over the sin offering. The following verse speaks of that vessel:

"*Then for the unclean person they shall take some of the ashes of the burnt purification from sin and flowing water shall be added to them in a vessel.*" (Num.19:17).

The use of the Greek word *loutron* in a verse which speaks of the new birth (Titus 3:5) demonstrates that the reference to "water" at John 3:5 is in regard to the water of purification of Numbers 19 and not water baptism. In the following passage we can see another place where the Apostle Paul used the word *loutron*:

The Washing of Water by the Word

"*Husbands, love your wives, just as Christ also loved the church and gave Himself up for her, so that He might sanctify her, having cleansed her by* **the washing (loutron) of water with the word**," (Eph.5:25-26).

At Ephesians 5:25-26 Paul is using the words "the washing of water" in a typical sense, meaning that the Jews received the benefits of the sin-offering by the water and those in the church receive the benefits of the death of the Lord Jesus with the "word"--"*the washing of water with the word.*"

Anderson wrote, "We know what the sacrifice typified, what

77

did the water typify? What is the means by which the defiled sinner is brought into contact, as it were, with the great sin offering of Calvary? By 'the word of the truth of the gospel.'" [5]

Born Again By the Word of God

From this we can know that in "type" the water signifies the "word" and it is the word of God by which the believing sinner is born again:

"***Being born again***, *not of corruptible seed, but of incorruptible,* ***by the word of God***...*And* ***this is the word which by the gospel is preached unto you***" (1 Pet.1:23, 25).

"***Of his own will begat he us with the word of truth***, *that we should be a kind of firstfruits of his creatures*" (Jas.1:18).

One Birth

Let us look at the following passage:

"*Jesus answered, 'Truly, truly, I say to you, unless one is born of water and the Spirit he cannot enter into the kingdom of God. That which is born of the flesh is flesh, and that which is born of the Spirit is spirit. Do not be amazed that I said to you, 'You must be born again. The wind blows where it wishes and you hear the sound of it, but do not know where it comes from and where it is going; so is everyone who is born of the Spirit'*"(Jn.3:5-8).

Anderson writes that "*first it is essential to notice that this is not a 'twofold' birth (of water, and of the Spirit), but emphatically 'one'--a birth of water-and-Spirit, in contrast with the birth which is of flesh... and the context emphasises it, for in the very next sentence, and again in verse 8, the water is omitted altogether, and the new man is spoken of merely as 'born of the Spirit.'*" [6]

Robert V. McCabe agrees, writing that "*in v. 5 the preposition 'ek' governs two nouns, 'hydor' and 'pneuma,' that are coordinated by 'kai.' This indicates that Jesus regards 'hydor kai pneuma' as a conceptual unity. If 'hydor kai pneuma' is a conceptual unity, this phrase may be taken either as a 'water-spirit' source or a 'water-and-Spirit' source of birth. A good case can be presented for either view in the context of John 3:1-8. With either view, there is one birth that is characterized either as 'water-spirit,' or 'water-and-Spirit.' Neither of these understandings suggest that there are two births, physical and spiritual*" [emphasis added]. [7]

The following verses demonstrate that the gospel comes not in word only but it is accompanied with the Holy Spirit:

"*It was revealed to them that they were not serving themselves, but you, in these things which now have been announced to you through those who preached the gospel to you by the Holy Spirit sent from heaven - things into which angels long to look*" (1 Pet.1:12).

"*for our gospel did not come to you in word only, but also in power and in the Holy Spirit and with full conviction; just as you know what kind of men we proved to be among you for your sake*" (1 Thess.1:5).

Ezekiel 36-37

Sir Robert sums up his conclusions in the following manner:

"*The water of John iii. does not refer to baptism: the question remains, What is its symbolism ? Here we must keep prominently in view that the truth involved ought to have been known to Nicodemus. 'Art thou the teacher of Israel, and knowest not these things?' the Lord exclaimed in indignant wonder at his ignorance. Therefore in speaking of the new birth by water and the Spirit the Lord referred to some distinctive truth of the Old Testament*

Scriptures, which ought to have been familiar to a Rabbi of the Sanhedrin....With this to guide us, we turn to one of the most definite of the prophecies, Ezek. xxxvi., xxxvii. We there read: 'I .. take you from among the heathen, and gather you of all countries, and will bring you into your own. Then will I sprinkle clean water upon you. . . . A heart also will I give you. . . . And I will put My Spirit within you.' Then follows the vision of the valley of dry bones. The prophet is commanded to say, 'thus saith the Lord God, Come from the four winds, O breath, and breathe upon these slain, that they may live.'

"*Here then is the most characteristic of all the prophecies of that great revival which the Lord's own lips have described as the 'regeneration'--a prophecy to which the Jew clung with special earnestness, a prophecy ignorance of which in a Rabbi of the Sanhedrin was a disgraceful as if an English theologian knew nothing of the Nicodemus sermon! And it was the great truth of this prophecy--salvation through the sin-offering in the power of the Divine Spirit, that the Lord enforced in His words to Nicodemus, and which the Apostle emphasised in th Epistle to Titus. Thus only could the sinner enter the Kingdom.*" [8]

Next, we read Anderson's explanation of the "typical" teaching in regard to the 37th chapter of Ezekiel, which speaks of the regeneration of the nation of Israel:

"*You ask, how can sinners, helpless, hopeless, dead--as dead as dry bones scattered upon the earth - be born again to God. 'Can these bones live?' is the question of Ezekiel 37: And the answer comes 'Prophesy unto these bones, and say unto them, O ye dry bones, hear the word of the Lord.' Preach to dead, lost sinners call upon them to hear the word of the Lord. This is man's part. Or if there be anything more, it is, 'Prophesy unto the Breath. Pray that the Spirit may breathe upon these slain that they may live.' The rest is God's work altogether, for 'the Spirit breathes where He wills.' Not that there is anything arbitrary in His working. God is never arbitrary; but He is always Sovereign. Men preach; the Spirit breathes; and the dry bones live. Thus it is that sinners are born again to God."* [9]

End Notes

1. Sir Robert Anderson, *The Bible or the Church?* (London: Pickering & Inglis, Second Edition), 225.
2. *Ibid.*
3. Ada R. Habershon, *Study of the Types*, (Grand Rapids: Kregel Publications, 1993, 75.
4. Sir Robert Anderson, *The Bible or the Church?*, 224.
5. *Ibid.*, 227.
6. *Ibid.*, 222-23.
7. Robert V. McCabe, "The Meaning of 'Born of Water and the Spirit' in John 3:5," *Detroit Baptist Seminary Journal* (Fall 1999), 85-107.
8. Sir Robert Anderson, *The Bible or the Church?*, 226-227.
9. Sir Robert Anderson, *Redemption Truths* (Grand Rapids: Kregel Classics, 1980), 137-38.

Appendix #2: "Law" or "the Law" at Romans 5:13?

The following translation of Romans 5:13-14 has been the source of much confusion for Christian theologians:

"*For until **the law** sin was in the world: but sin is not imputed when there is no law. Nevertheless death reigned from Adam to Moses, even over them that had not sinned after the similitude of Adam's transgression, who is the figure of him that was to come*" (Ro.5:13-14; KJV).

The following interpretation of these verses comes from William Barclay:

"*The law did not come until the time of Moses. Now, if there is no law, there can be no breach of the law; that is to say, there can be no sin. Therefore, the men who lived between Adam and Moses did in fact commit sinful actions, but they could not be counted as sinners, for the law did not yet exist.*

"*In spite of the fact that sin could not be reckoned to them, they still died. Death reigned over them, although they could not be accused of breaking a non-existent law.*

"*Why, then, did they die? It was because they had sinned in Adam. Their involvment in his sin caused their deaths, although there was no law for them to break. That, in fact, is Paul's proof that all men did sin in Adam.*" [1]

Barclay said there was no law for those who lived between Adam and Moses to break but the Scriptures tell a different story. In the following verse we can see that the Lord spoke of the "sin" committed by those of Sodom and Gomorrah and that happened before "the law" came into existence:

"*And the LORD said, Because the cry of Sodom and Gomorrah is great, and because **their sin is very grievous**"*

83

(Gen.18:20).

The fate of these ungodly men who lived in those cities bears witness to the fact that their sins were indeed imputed into their account:

"*Even as Sodom and Gomorrha, and the cities about them in like manner, giving themselves over to fornication, and going after strange flesh,* **are set forth for an example, suffering the vengeance of eternal fire**" (Jude 7).

John Calvin understood that sin was indeed imputed to men before "the law" came into existence, writing that "*before the law iniquities were by God imputed to men is evident from the punishment of Cain, from the deluge by which the whole world was destroyed, from the fate of Sodom, and from the plagues inflicted on Pharaoh and Abimelech on account of Abraham, and also from the plagues brought on the Egyptians.*" [2]

The following translation of the same verses serves to begin to clear up this confusion:

"***for until law sin was in the world***; *but sin is not put to account when there is no law; but death reigned from Adam until Moses, even upon those who had not sinned in the likeness of Adam's transgression, who is the figure of him to come*" (Ro.5:13-14; DBY).

Here we see that there is no definite article ('the') before the Greek word translated "law." How is the word "law" to be understood here? Beginning in the second chapter of this epistle Paul speaks of "law" as being in regard to the "moral law" as revealed by either "the law" of Moses or by the "conscience." Here we see a reference to the only "moral law" which was universally known between Adam and the giving of "the law" by Moses:

"*For when* **the Gentiles, which have not the law**, *do by nature the things contained in the law, these, having not the law, are a law unto themselves:* **Which shew the work of the law written in** *their hearts, their conscience also bearing witness*" (Ro.2:14-15).

The Definite Article

John F. Walvoord, the second President of Dallas Theological Seminary, offers the following concerning the presence or the absence of the definite article before the Greek word translated "law":

It is obvious that there must be some meaning to the use of the article or its absence, particularly when we observe careful distinction often in the same verse of Scripture. It is the writer's contention that the article when used has some significance, and when it is not used there must be some reason for its absence. He (Paul) therefore concludes in 3:20 that 'by the deeds of the law shall no flesh be justified.' ***As the 'law' includes both Jews and Gentiles in this summary, it is clear that it has the general meaning of any moral law***" [emphasis added]. [3]

Of course the only "moral law" which men were responsible for keeping in a universal sense between Adam and the giving of the law by Moses was the law written in men's heart, the same law of which the conscience bears witness.

Later in the same journal Walvoord says the same thing in regard to Romans 10:4-5: "*In both instances 'nomos' occurs without the article. In the first instance, in vs. 4, it seems clear that **the reference is to any moral law**. The argument is that Christ is the end of all law, as far as law resulting in righteousness is concerned*" [emphasis added]. [4]

End Notes

1. William Barclay, *The Daily Study Bible Series: The Letter to the Romans*; Revised Edition (Philadelphia: The Westminster Press, 1975), 81.

2. John Calvin, Commentary on Romans 5:13; Accessed August 26, 2018, https://www.studylight.org/commentaries/cal/romans-5.html

3. John F. Walvoord, "Law in the Epistle to the Romans," *Bibliotheca Sacra*, Jan., 1937, (Vol. 94, #373), 17,21.

4. John F. Walvoord, "Law in the Epistle to the Romans," *Bibliotheca Sacra*, July-Sept., 1937; (Vol.94, #375), 286.

Appendix #3: Was Romans 5:12-14 a Riddle in the First Century?

There are reasons to believe that those who originally received the epistle to the Romans understood that all people who lived between Adam and Moses died spiritually when they sinned against their consciences and that Adam was responsible for the fact that all people have a conscience. So when they read Romans 5:12 they would have known immediately how Adam was responsible for all people dying spiritually when they sinned.

Robert Yarbrough said that "*Paul's offhand mention of Adam presupposes that his Corinthian readers would have been familiar with the Genesis 1-3 narrative. It is evident, E. Schnabel writes,* **that in Paul's instruction of Jesus-believers in Corinth some three years previously he had taught them 'the Old Testament account of creation and the fall'**" [emphasis added].[1]

It is entirely possible that it was common knowledge within the church at Corinth that when Adam ate of the Tree of the Knowledge of Good and Evil that event resulted in all people having a consciousness of the law which is written in their heart. And it is entirely possible that knowledge would find its way to Rome since many in that church were Paul's converts or or associates from other parts of the empire. John Witmer writes that Paul's "*numerous greetings to individuals (28 persons are named or referred to, plus several groups) reveal the impact of Paul's ministry on the establishment and the devolopment of the church at Rome. Many of the believers there were Paul's converts or associates in other parts of the empire.*"[2]

There is certainly good reasons to suppose that Paul knew that those in the church at Rome were aware that Adam's sin brought a conscience to all people and that explains why he didn't go into more detail at Romans 5.

So we can understand that Paul's offhand mention of Adam at Romans 5:12 presupposes that his readers from the church at Rome would have been familiar with the Genesis 1-3 narrative. With all of these things in mind it is not difficult to understand that Paul would take it for granted that those who received this epistle would know immediately that he was speaking of people dying spiritually when they sinned against their conscience and that Adam was responsible for all of his posterity having a conscience.

"*For this cause, even as **by one man sin entered into the world**, and by sin death; and thus death passed upon all men, **for that all have sinned: for until law sin was in the world; but sin is not put to account when there is no law; but death reigned from Adam until Moses**, even upon those who had not sinned in the likeness of Adam's transgression, who is the figure of him to come*" (Ro.5:12-14; DBY).

By the time when Augustine developed his theory of Original Sin many teachings of the first century church had been lost and one of them was the idea that Adam's sin resulted in all people having a conscience.

End Notes

1. Robert W. Yarbrough, "Adam in the New Testament," in *Adam, the Fall, and Original Sin*, 46.
2. John A. Witmer, *The Bible Knowledge Commentary; New Testament*, 436.

Appendix #4: There is None Righteous, No, Not One

John Calvin wrote the following in an effort to try to prove that the whole posterity of Adam has been corrupted:

"*The Apostle, when he would humble man's pride, uses these words:* **'There is none righteous, no, not one**: *there is none that understandeth, there is none that seeketh after God. They are all gone out of the way, they are together become unprofitable; there is none that does good, no, not one. Their throat is an open sepulchre; with their tongues they have used deceit; the poison of asps is under their lips: Whose mouth is full of cursing and bitterness: their feet are swift to shed blood: destruction and misery are in their ways: and the way of peace have they not known: there is no fear of God before their eyes,' (Rom. 3: 10-18.) Thus he thunders not against certain individuals,* **but against the whole posterity of Adam** - *not against the depraved manners of any single age, but the perpetual corruption of nature*" [*emphasis added*]. [1]

When we look at the verse which precedes the ones which Calvin quoted we can understand that those whom Paul says are "under sin" are spoken about in the previous chapters:

"*What then? are we better than they? No, in no wise:* **for we have before proved both Jews and Gentiles, that they are all under sin**; *As it is written, There is none righteous, no, not one*" (Ro.3:9-10).

In his commentary on this verse Joseph Benson wrote: "*For we have before proved - Namely, in the two former chapters; both Jews -* **By the breach of the written law; and Gentiles -** **By transgressing the law of nature**; *that they are all - Every one of them, without exception; under sin - Under the guilt and power of it.*" [2]

According to Benson all are under sin because of their own sin and not because of the sin of Adam.

In the previous chapters we can see that all people are under sin because of their own sin:

"*For as many as have sinned without law shall also perish without law: and as many as have sinned in the law shall be judged by the law*" (Ro.2:12).

In regard to Romans 2:12 Thomas Schreiner writes that "*For he (Paul) clearly says in 2:12 that those without the law perish because they violate the law written on their heart.* **Paul does not argue in chapter 2 that Adam's sin is their basis for their judgment.** *They perished because they contravened God's moral norms*" [*emphasis added*]. ³

Those who Paul says are "under sin" are that way because of their own sin and not because of the sin of Adam. And since infants and little children have not yet sinned they are not under sin so there is no such thing as a "corruption" of all of Adam's posterity.

End Notes

1. John Calvin, *Institutes of the Christian Religion: Books First and Second* (North Charleston, NC: Createspace), 188.

2. Joseph Benson, *Benson Commentary on the Old and New Testaments*; Accessed September 2, 2008, http://biblehub.com/commentaries/benson/romans/3.htm

3. Thomas R. Schreiner, *Adam, The Fall, and Original sin*, 280.

Appendix #5: The Flesh Lusteth Against the Spirit

Augustine quoted the following passage in his attempt to try to prove that the physical body of all people emerge from the womb with defects:

"*For **the flesh lusteth against the Spirit**, and the Spirit against the flesh: and these are contrary the one to the other: so that ye cannot do the things that ye would*" (Gal.5:17).

From the context we can see that Paul is speaking about a Christian's walk:

"*This I say then, Walk in the Spirit, and ye shall not fulfil the lust of the flesh*" (Gal.5:16).

When Paul contrasts walking in the Spirit with walking in the flesh he is speaking of living a God-centered life as opposed to living a self-centered life.

The following verse also speaks of the Christian's walk:

"*So then they that are in the flesh cannot please God*" (Ro.8:8).

In his commentary on this verse John Calvin says that "*those who give themselves up to be guided by the lusts of the flesh, are all of them abominable before God; and he has thus far confirmed this truth, --that all who walk not after the Spirit are alienated from Christ, **for they are without any spiritual life***" [emphasis added] [1]

According to Calvin this verse is speaking about the unsaved. R.C. Sproul is of the same mind, writing the following:

"***Fallen man is flesh. In the flesh he can do nothing to please God**. Paul declares, 'The fleshly mind is enmity against God; for it is not subject to the law of God, nor indeed can be. So* *then, those who are in the flesh cannot please God' (Rom. 8:7, 8)."* [2]

Again, these verses are speaking of a Christian's "walk." A Christian can either walk after the Spirit or after the flesh:

"That the righteousness of the law might be fulfilled in us, who walk not after the flesh, but after the Spirit" (Ro.8:4).

Paul speaks about that same principle in the verse which follows:

"For they that are after the flesh do mind the things of the flesh; but they that are after the Spirit the things of the Spirit" (Ro.8:5).

We can also understand that it is indeed possible for a Christian to walk or live after the flesh because Paul tells Christians that if they live after the flesh they shall die:

"For if ye live after the flesh, ye shall die: but if ye through the Spirit do mortify the deeds of the body, ye shall live" (Ro.8:13).

On this subject Douglas Moo writes that "*what is especially important is to trace the connection between 'flesh' and human sin.* **The natural human condition is to be 'in the flesh,' to be fundamentally determined by the perspective of this world, in contrast to the world to come.** *And sin is the inevitable result of this condition...Christians, because they are still in this world, must strive to avoid falling into such patterns of thought and activity (**8:12-13**; 13:14)*" [emphasis added] [3]

If it is impossible that a Christian can walk after the flesh then it would make absolutely no sense for Paul to tell Christians that "if they live after the flesh you shall die."

The "death" spoken of here is in regard to the Christian's walk, that "*we should also walk in newness of life*" (Ro.6:4) so that "*the life also of Jesus might be made manifest in our mortal flesh*" (2 Cor.4:11). The second part of verse 13 is telling Christians that if they mortify the deeds of the body they will live. Christians are already received eternal life so Paul's words there are also referring to walking in newness of life.

From all of this we can understand that Christians can indeed walk in the flesh and when they live or walk that way they cannot please God. The Apostle John refers to that kind of walk as walking in darkness:

*"This then is the message which we have heard of him, and declare unto you, that God is light, and in him is no darkness at all. If we say that we have fellowship with him, **and walk in darkness**, we lie, and do not the truth"* (1 Jn.1:5-6).

Matthew Henry wrote the following commentary about Romans 8:8:

*"Believers may be chastened of the Lord, but will not be condemned with the world. By their union with Christ through faith, they are thus secured. **What is the principle of their walk; the flesh or the Spirit, the old or the new nature, corruption or grace?** For which of these do we make provision, by which are we governed?"* [*emphasis added*] [4]

Sir Robert Anderson writes, *"This verse is used to support the dogma that, because of the Fall, man's nature is so utterly depraved that he is incapable of leading a moral and upright life. As the Westminster Divines express it, 'We are utterly indisposed, disabled, and made opposite to all good.' This theology obviously impugns the righteousness of God in punishing men for their sins. In fact, it represents Him as a tyrant who punishes the lame for limping and the blind for losing their way"* [5]

End Notes

1. John Calvin, Commentary at Romans 8:8; Accessed September 3, 2018, https://www.studylight.org/commentaries/cal/romans-8.html

2. R. C. Sproul, *John 3:16 and Man's Ability to Choose God*; Accessed September 3, 2018, https://www.ligonier.org/blog/mans-ability-choose-god/

3. Douglas J. Moo, *Fallen: A Theology of Sin*, 120.

4. Matthew Henry, *Concise Commentary on the Whole Bible*; Accessed September2, 2018, http://biblehub.com/commentaries/mhc/romans/8.htm

5. Sir Robert Anderson, *Misundersood Texts of the New Testament*, 75.

Appendix #6: By Nature the Children of Wrath

John Calvin wrote that "*the only explanation which can be given of the expression, 'in Adam all died,' is, that he by sinning not only brought disaster and ruin upon himself, but also **plunged our nature into like destruction**; and that not only in one fault, in a matter not pertaining to us, but **by the corruption into which he himself fell, he infected his whole seed**. Paul never could have said that all are '**by nature the children of wrath**,' (Eph. 2:3), if they had not been cursed from the womb*" [*emphasis added*]. [1]

In his remarks on the phrase "children of wrath" Calvin denied that anyone is created by God that way. "*Paul never could have said that all are 'by nature the children of wrath,' (Eph. 2:3),*" said Calvin, " *if they had not been cursed from the womb.* **And it is obvious that the nature there referred to is not nature such as God created**, *but as vitiated in Adam;* **for it would have been most incongruous to make God the author of death**" [*emphasis added*]. [2]

Calvin is right when he says that the LORD does not create children in that manner. No one becomes what can be described as being "a child of wrath" until he sins:

"*Wherein in time past **ye walked according to the course of this world, according to the prince of the power of the air**, the spirit that now worketh in the children of disobedience: Among whom also we all had our conversation in times past in the lusts of our flesh, **fulfilling the desires of the flesh and of the mind; and were by nature the children of wrath**, even as others*" (Eph.2:2-3).

End Notes

1. John Calvin, *Institutes of the Christian Religion: Books First and Second*, 162.
2. John Calvin, *Institutes of the Christian Religion*, translated by Henry Beveridge (Peabody, MA: Hendrickson Publishers, 2008), 151.

Appendix #7: In Sin Did My Mother Conceive Me

John Calvin wrote that "*Surely there is no ambiguity in David's confession, 'I was shapen in iniquity; and in sin did my mother conceive me,' (Ps. 51:5). His object in the passage is not to throw blame on his parents; but the better to commend the goodness of God towards him, he properly reiterates the confession of impurity from his very birth*"[emphasis added]. [1]

Let us look at the context where these words are found:

"*Have mercy upon me, O God, according to thy lovingkindness: according unto the multitude of thy tender mercies blot out my transgressions. Wash me throughly from mine iniquity, and cleanse me from my sin. For I acknowledge my transgressions: and my sin is ever before me. Against thee, thee only, have I sinned, and done this evil in thy sight: that thou mightest be justified when thou speakest, and be clear when thou judgest. Behold, **I was shapen in iniquity; and in sin did my mother conceive me**. Behold, thou desirest truth in the inward parts: and in the hidden part thou shalt make me to know wisdom. **Purge me with hyssop, and I shall be clean: wash me, and I shall be whiter than snow.** Make me to hear joy and gladness; **that the bones which thou hast broken may rejoice**"* (Ps.51:1-8).

In this passage David was using figurative language while confessing to the LORD his deep sense of guilt for his sin. When we examine the context where David speaks of being conceived in sin we see that David employed figurative language numerous times, or else we must believe that God breaks the bones of people when they sin or that the broken bones rejoice when forgiven.

Again we must look at what David said at another place about how He was created by God:

"*For thou hast possessed my reins: thou hast covered me in my mother's womb. **I will praise thee; for I am fearfully and wonderfully made**: marvellous are thy works; and that my soul knoweth right well*" (Ps.139:13-14).

We also know that David's son Solomon wrote that God created mankind upright (Eccl.7:29; NIV).

Albert Barnes wrote that "*the idea here is not to cast reflections on the character of his mother, or to refer to her feelings in regard to his conception and birth, but the design is to express **his deep sense of his own depravity**; a depravity so deep as to demonstrate that it must have had its origin in the very beginning of his existence*" [*emphasis added*]. [2]

The following words of the Lord Jesus about "little children" prove that He did not believe that little children are conceived in sin:

"*Then people brought little children to Jesus for him to place his hands on them and pray for them. But the disciples rebuked them. Jesus said, 'Let the little children come to me, and do not hinder them, **for the kingdom of heaven belongs to such as these**'*" (Mt.19:13-14; NIV).

According to the theory of Original Sin infants and little children are spiritually dead and therefore cannot enter the kingdom of God but the Lord says that the kingdom belongs to them.

End Notes

1. John Calvin, *Institutes of the Christian Religion*, translated by Henry Beveridge (Peabody, MA: Hendrickson Publishers, 2008), 150.

2. Albert Barnes, *Notes on the Bible*; Accessed September 3, 2018, http://biblehub.com/commentaries/barnes/psalms/51.htm

The author encourages edifying discussion regarding this book. Please contact him via email at jerryshugart2@yahoo.com

MORE BIBLICAL INSTRUCTION FROM GERALD B. SHUGART

Last Days Fables

Eschatology - the Bible is incredibly clear on most components of the subject.

However, many Bible scholars attempt to muddy the waters regarding the study of the last days of this age by adhering to a flawed basic interpretation of the Bible.

In so doing, those individuals miss the mark of Biblical truth as God intended man to understand it while causing confusion and concern amongst the masses - even Christians. This is a cycle of failure that perpetuates error and bewilderment for many who search for accurate information pertaining to the future - according to the Word of God.

Author and Bible teacher Gerald B. Shugart presents the truth of God's Word plainly herein to guide readers away from confusion and error and into a place of information, accuracy and contentedness in the Lord and His perfect plan.

If you find yourself desiring to have a more complete understanding of eschatology (the study of the future period described commonly as "the last days"), follow along with the author as he provides Biblical truth and guidance in a simple to understand manner.

ALSO AVAILABLE FROM GERALD B. SHUGART

SIR ROBERT ANDERSON - The Thinking Man's Guide to the Bible

Biblical insight by the real life Sherlock Holmes who solved the "Jack the Ripper" case.

Sir Robert Anderson, KCB (29 May 1841 – 15 November 1918), was the Chief of the Criminal Investigation Departament of Scotland Yard from 1888 to 1901. He was also an intelligence officer, theologian and writer.

Author Gerald B. Shugart presents an intriguing historical panorama of the Biblical studies and spiritual insight of Sir Robert Anderson, the individual responsible for the investigation of the man known the world over as "Jack the Ripper" in Victorian-era London. Fully referenced.

Gerald Shugart's books are available in both Kindle and print format. Print copies are available wherever books are sold.

www.ingramcontent.com/pod-product-compliance
Lightning Source LLC
Chambersburg PA
CBHW032049090426

42744CB00004B/141